The Global Classroom

The Global Classroom
An Essential Guide
to Study Abroad

Jeffrey S. Lantis, Ph.D.
Professor of Political Science
The College of Wooster

Jessica DuPlaga
Director of Off-Campus Studies
The College of Wooster

Paradigm Publishers
Boulder • London

Copyright © 2010 Paradigm Publishers

Published in the United States by Paradigm Publishers, 3360 Mitchell Lane, Suite E, Boulder, CO 80301 USA.

Paradigm Publishers is the trade name of Birkenkamp & Company, LLC, Dean Birkenkamp, President and Publisher.

Library of Congress Cataloging-in-Publication Data
Lantis, Jeffrey S., 1966–
    The global classroom : an essential guide to study abroad / Jeffrey S. Lantis and Jessica DuPlaga.
        p. cm. — (International studies intensives series)
    Includes bibliographical references and index.
    ISBN 978-1-59451-676-4 (hardcover : alk. paper)
    ISBN 978-1-59451-677-1 (hardcover : alk. paper
    1. International education.   I. DuPlaga, Jessica.   II. Title.
    LC1090.L279 2010
    370.116—dc22
                        2009036131

Printed and bound in the United States of America on acid-free paper that meets the standards of the American National Standard for Permanence of Paper for Printed Library Materials.

14 13 12 11 10   1 2 3 4 5

To my parents, Paul and Patricia Lantis,
who have inspired me to explore the world.
—J. S. L.

To my mother, and to the many educators in my life,
who believed in me and encouraged me to take on
challenges I never thought I would be able to conquer.
—J. D.

CONTENTS

PREFACE AND ACKNOWLEDGMENTS

Touring the Kremlin on a crisp autumn day. Sipping coffee at an outdoor café in Paris. Talking with professors at the Australian National University in Canberra. Hunting for bargains at a local market in Jamaica. Hiking up the side of a mountain in the Scottish highlands. Talking with students at the University of Brasilia. Craning our necks to view the beauty of the Sistine Chapel in Rome during an art history lecture. Walking along the path where the Berlin Wall once divided a city, a country, and the world. These are the experiences of our lives. They are both personal and educational. They have transformed us, as similar experiences have shaped the lives of millions of other students from the United States.

This book is about preparing students to meaningfully study abroad—to view the preparation for overseas study, participation in an academically rigorous program, and the return home as parts of a holistic intellectual and emotional journey. By drawing on prominent theories of learning and cross-cultural education, the book builds the discussion around a contemporary *academic development* approach to contextualizing knowledge about study abroad. In other words, this book gives students, faculty, and study abroad professionals the tools they need to help position the study abroad experience in a valuable academic context.

The organizational plan of the book reflects a very practical orientation that should appeal to a broad audience. It takes students step by step from their first thoughts about the possibility of study abroad all the way to marketing their knowledge as engaged global citizens to future employers. In addition to covering all phases of education abroad, it includes resources and worksheets for easy use by students, faculty, and advisers. The book offers flexibility in application depending on the institution, curricular orientation, or personal interests.

* * *

The authors would like to recognize many people who helped make this book possible. First, we are grateful to the hundreds of students with whom we have worked for their enthusiasm about study abroad. Their questions, experiences, and ideas serve as inspiration for this book. We also thank our colleagues at The College of Wooster for their encouragement and interest in the project. President Grant Cornwell and Interim Provost Shila Garg have helped to shape our understanding of the power of crossing cultures and of global citizenship. In addition, Kent Kille, Katie Holt, Nicola Kille, Virginia Wickline, Harry Gamble, and many others provided valuable ideas. We also have benefited from participation in professional conferences and programs sponsored by the Forum on Education Abroad (including its flagship journal, *Frontiers: The Interdisciplinary Journal of Study Abroad*) and NAFSA: Association of International Educators.

Jeffrey Lantis is grateful for opportunities to teach and research in locales as diverse as Brasília, Moscow, Bonn, and Sydney. In 2007, Lantis received a J. William Fulbright Senior Scholar Award to serve as a Visiting Scholar in the Department of International Relations in the Research School of Pacific and Asian Studies at the Australian National University and the School of Social Sciences and International Studies at the University of New South Wales. He thanks colleagues in both programs and especially the Fulbright Commission staff, including Mark Darby and Lyndell Wilson, for their sponsorship. The Fulbright commitment to the promotion of international educational and cultural exchange was a strong inspiration for this project. In addition, Lantis acknowledges valuable research and editorial assistance from Elysia Tonti, Tess Morrissey, and Whitney Louderback.

Jessica DuPlaga would like to thank colleagues at the Institute for the International Education of Students (IES) for providing the opportunity to enter into the world of study abroad, first as a student and later as a professional. Her time abroad was an inspiration for her personal and professional development. Chantal Rouchet, Thibaut de Berranger, and Béatrice de la Bretesche at the IES Center in Nantes, France, provided endless encouragement and examples of student-centered advising and administration that have shaped DuPlaga's vision of education and study abroad. She also acknowledges the personal, academic, and professional encouragement of past and current teachers and colleagues—Betty Ford, Carolyn Durham, Nicola Kille, and many others.

Finally, the authors owe a special debt of gratitude to Jennifer Knerr and members of the Editorial Board of the International Studies Intensives Series at Paradigm for their encouragement on the project. We appreciate input on the project from James McCormick, Dan Caldwell, Cooper Drury, Robin Broad, David Skidmore, Steve Hook, and others. We are also grateful for helpful comments from anonymous reviewers. Their suggestions helped us to refine the focus of the project. While this book is the product of a collaborative process, we remain responsible for any errors of argument or omission in the text.

—*Jeffrey S. Lantis and Jessica DuPlaga*

Chapter One
GETTING STARTED:
WHY STUDY ABROAD?

Congratulations! You are planning to embark on an exciting and enriching study abroad experience. This book is designed to help you prepare for and get the most from study abroad as part of a holistic educational plan. By linking each phase of your journey to critical academic objectives, the book provides a useful context for a meaningful study abroad experience. It also features helpful exercises and reviews a number of practical themes for you to consider before, during, and after your time abroad. Put simply, this book gives you many of the tools you will need to succeed.

Study abroad can be an enriching component of any educational program and can transform your view of the world, others, and even yourself.[1] As practitioners know, if you are well prepared to study abroad you are much more likely to benefit from the experience. Yet both students and faculty members are sometimes less attuned to academic preparation for study abroad than they should be. With nearly 250,000 U.S. college students studying abroad each year, it is especially important to reflect meaningfully on the value of the experience.[2] In fact, the number of students engaged in education abroad is expected to grow exponentially in the coming decade. Some legislators want to facilitate study abroad for *one million U.S. undergraduate students per year by 2017*. The federal government is also working with colleges and universities to increase participation of underrepresented students in education abroad.[3]

These changes are welcome in the post–September 11 world. In 2001 many professionals feared that the rate of overseas study would

Figure 1.1   The Global Classroom Learning Cycle

decline in the wake of concerns about terrorism at home and abroad. Today we can say that this never materialized. While the numbers of foreign students attending U.S. colleges and universities dipped slightly after 2001, they have now recovered. Indeed, there are now record numbers of students studying abroad; we are witnessing incredible growth in curiosity about the world among today's college students.[4] If you study abroad, you are part of this important wave of global engagement.

The Global Classroom learning cycle model illustrates the importance of viewing the study abroad experience holistically as an educational journey centered on critical academic objectives. In this chapter we explore key themes to get you started, including the philosophy behind overseas study and the potential values of the experience. Later in the book, we address choosing the right program, preparation for study abroad, and active engagement in foreign communities and cultures. The book also features chapters devoted to reorientation and exploring pathways for integrating the experience into undergraduate and graduate education and careers as engaged global citizens. In essence, this book provides both a primer for orienting study abroad within a larger educational program and a practical guide to address issues that will arise during the experience.

A Brief History of Study Abroad

Your plan to study abroad is part of a centuries-old tradition in liberal learning. In nineteenth-century Europe, for example, landowning families typically sent their teenage sons and daughters abroad as a formative educational experience. Some viewed it as a necessary rite of passage from childhood to maturity. The concept of university and college support for study abroad became much more institutionalized, and democratized, in the twentieth century. The National Association of Foreign Student Advisors (NAFSA) was created in 1948 to help foster this expanding dimension of college education. Look around today and you will find that most colleges and universities celebrate the value of transcultural knowledge through international education.[5] Clearly, international education has come of age.

Today, study abroad has become ingrained in our understanding of what it means to be an educated and responsible citizen of the world. For example, former president Bill Clinton studied at Oxford University as a Rhodes scholar. Kofi Annan, former secretary-general of the United Nations, was an international student from Ghana who graduated from Macalaster College in Minnesota. In 2007–2008, more than 600,000 international students enrolled in U.S. colleges and universities.[6] President Barack Obama may be the quintessential foreign-educated U.S. student: born in the United States to an American mother and a Kenyan father, Obama attended school for eight years in Indonesia, then moved to Hawaii to finish high school. After graduating from Harvard Law School, Obama became a community organizer in inner-city Chicago and worked closely with civic leaders and immigrant groups from all over the world. Each of these individuals became more culturally sensitive and knowledgeable about the world through their experiences, empowering them to consider ways to help solve global problems.

So, you are not the first student to study abroad, and you will not be the last. It is fascinating to think of your upcoming journey as part of a long-standing educational tradition—the "Grand Tour" through study abroad. This is backed up by studies that show the incredible value of the experience. Benjamin Hadis argues that students typically grow personally and intellectually from the experience, gaining in curiosity and academic interest in the world. Indeed, they become "better students."[7] The emphasis in this book is consistent with prevailing trends in the higher education literature. It draws on contemporary scholarship about experiential learning and links themes to an academic core to better contextualize how you can learn more about yourself, other cultures and societies, and global challenges.[8]

Why Do You Want to Study Abroad?

Most discussions of study abroad begin with *where* you want to go. But we think that a much more fascinating place to start this dialogue is with *why* you want to study abroad. Indeed, the global classroom starts with *you*. Learning more about who you are may be the key to understanding your motivations in relation to the academic objectives of the experience. We suggest four major dimensions of the global classroom experience: personal identity, cultural identity, vocational development, and global citizenship (see Figure 1.2). These may offer a useful guide for framing your educational journey.

Learning About Yourself and the World

Students typically learn a great deal about the world through study abroad, but they may learn as much or more about *themselves* through the experience. We say this confidently based on our own experiences with study abroad and thousands of student testimonies to this effect.

Figure 1.2 Dimensions of the Global Classroom

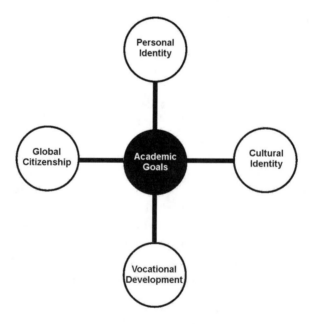

Why do *you* want to study abroad? Personal identity and orientation are often primary motivations for considering study abroad. By opening this book, you have identified yourself as someone who is profoundly curious about how the rest of the world works—and may be exploring ways to translate your interest into action. Overseas study will provide you with an opportunity to reflect critically on your own identity as much as that of others. This means consideration of who you are in terms of social and psychological orientation, as well as how you see the world around you.

"Before You Go—Dimensions of the Global Classroom Experience" (see Worksheet 1) provides you with a special opportunity to reflect critically on questions such as:

- Why do you want to study abroad?
- What do you hope to gain from the experience on a personal level? What sort of experiences do you want to have?
- What do you want to *learn*? Do you want to learn about a particular culture or language? Are you looking for a learning experience that you cannot have at your home institution?
- Why are you curious about other regions or countries of the world?
- Do you consider yourself to be open-minded?
- Do you identify yourself as someone who can make a difference in the world?
- Are you generally optimistic or pessimistic?
- What worries or concerns do you have about logistics or adaptation?
- Are you multilingual?
- Are you environmentally conscious?
- Do you relate well to others? Are you flexible? Do you adapt easily to new circumstances?
- How do you picture yourself using this experience when you return? At your home institution? Professionally?

Seeking answers to these questions in advance of your study abroad experience can help you ponder your own identity in relation to others, the potential links to your academic development, and the connection between study abroad and your larger educational and life plans. Experts Larry Braskamp, David Braskamp, and Kelly Merrill emphasize the importance of viewing study abroad as part of a larger developmental approach. They believe that everyone can gain cognitive, interpersonal, and intrapersonal maturity through experiences such as study abroad. In other words, people *grow* as they think about their sense of self, place, and their journey through life.[9]

Learning About Culture

What Do You Know About Your Own Culture?

The study abroad experience begins at home. The search for identity can be understood as the process of establishing boundaries for one's self and others. Identity also helps shape our sense of local, national, and global responsibilities. In political science classes, for example, we challenge students to think about the role of beliefs and ideologies in shaping policy-making processes. Place may also have an important role in affecting beliefs. For example in the United States, whether people live in a "red" or "blue" state may also reflect how they and their neighbors feel about issues such as universal health care, immigration policy, school funding, and the U.S. war on terror. Faculty members can also incorporate subjects vital to study abroad, like identity and culture, in class instruction in disciplines as diverse as psychology, art history, religious studies, and anthropology.

What is culture, after all? Culture is both simple and complex, both universal and subjective. The United Nations Educational, Scientific, and Cultural Organization (UNESCO) defines culture as the "set of distinctive spiritual, material, intellectual, and emotional features of society or a social group, and . . . it encompasses, in addition to art and literature, lifestyles, ways of living together, value systems, traditions, and beliefs."[10] Psychologists refer to culture as "a set of loosely organized ideas and practices produced and reproduced by a network of interconnected individuals."[11] Milton Bennett defines culture as "the learned and shared values, beliefs and behaviors of a group of interacting people."[12] Within these definitions one can begin to see the complexity of the term and its implications for a variety of academic disciplines. Ultimately, culture encompasses what we do, how we interact socially, what motivates us, and how we perceive the world and others.

Culture can be both *objective* and *subjective*. Objective culture includes "the artifacts and visions created by a group of interacting people, such as their political and economic systems, expressions in art, architecture, literature, and dance, heroes and holidays, and collective history." Subjective culture, on the other hand, includes the "psychological features that define a group of people—their everyday thinking and behavior."[13] Culture includes things that we can easily see and things we cannot see. Like an iceberg, the visible, objective features of culture are just a small part of the whole; nine-tenths of culture remains subjective, below the surface, not readily visible.[14]

As a U.S. student participating in a study abroad program you will find yourself instantly deputized as an "ambassador" of the United States. Many foreign citizens will be curious about your country (and will often know much more about issues in the United States than you do of their country or region). In preparation to serve as an unofficial cultural ambassador, it is important to reflect on how you feel about questions related to U.S. political and cultural identity, such as:

- How can you explain the racial divides and discrimination that still exist in the United States?
- What are you doing about global warming, especially since Americans consume so many of the world's natural resources?
- How do you feel about U.S. policy in Iraq and Afghanistan?
- Will it ever be possible for U.S. citizens to elect a woman as president?
- Oh, by the way, did you vote for Barack Obama? What do you think of your new president?

These are some of the many questions about U.S. politics and culture you are likely to hear when you interact with citizens of other countries.

One way to broaden your perspective is by looking at how the rest of the world views the United States. According to a recent poll of citizens from twenty-four countries, for example, many hold generally favorable views of the United States (measured as 40 percent favorability ratings or higher). Some of the most positive views toward the United States can be found in South Korea, India, and Poland; less positive views are found in Turkey, France, and Lebanon. It is also noteworthy that positive opinions were on the rise, with respondents expressing a widespread belief in 2008 "that U.S. foreign policy will change for the better" after the inauguration of President Obama.[15] In a similar poll of eleven countries, an average of 61 percent of respondents said U.S. science and technological innovation was a model for the rest of the world, and more than 70 percent expressed high regard for U.S. movies, popular music, and clothing. However, the vast majority polled *did not see the United States as a better country in which to live than their own*: 76 percent of the citizens from other countries polled said they preferred living in their home country to the prospect of moving to the United States.[16] Finally, in an interesting twist, polls show that many citizens of the world draw sharp distinctions between the American government and the American people. Most people surveyed have a very favorable opinion of Americans as individuals.[17]

You will most certainly be asked about U.S. culture and society when you are abroad. Your hosts are bound to be curious about the cultural identities, common practices and traditions, symbols, and controversies in the United States, due to the increasing diversity of our society. For example, would you describe U.S. society with regard to diversity as a "melting pot" or a "salad bowl"? Today, Los Angeles, California, has the same number of Spanish-language speakers as English-speakers. Immigrants and their children account for one in every five residents in the United States.[18] Some 18 percent of U.S. households speak languages other than English at home.[19] These realities lend to a special mix of diversity in terms of social norms, customs, traditions, religion, and language. We encourage you to ponder these and other dimensions of culture and society before you leave home.

What Do You Know About Foreign Cultures?
Studies show that the primary reason students want to study abroad is to learn about foreign cultures.[20] But what does this really mean? With nearly 200 independent countries in the world today and thousands of distinct national identities among and between them, the world presents an incredible learning laboratory of cultural diversity. Cultural differences may be manifest on at least three levels: national, group, and individual.

First, a national culture may be relatively easy to identify. Montserrat Guibernau defines national identity as "a collective sentiment based upon the belief of belonging to the same nation and of sharing most of the attributes that make it distinct from other nations." While noting that national identity can be fluid, it is often characterized by beliefs in a "common culture, history, kinship, language, religion, territory, founding moment and destiny."[21]

Conceptions of a national culture or identity also raise interesting questions about stereotypes. Take, for example, this set of characterizations: "The French love cheese and are proud of the Enlightenment and the changes brought about by the Revolution. The English enjoy cricket, tea, and the countryside. . . . U.S. citizens are proud of the founding fathers of their nation; they love steaks and big cars. Spaniards appreciate good wine and *paella* and are content about Columbus' discovery of America under Castilian sponsorship."[22] These are blatant stereotypes. A stereotype is the application of an idea of a commonality among members of a group, expressed through an oversimplified opinion, attitude, or judgment. It occurs "when we act as if all members of a culture or group share the same characteristics"; it can be positive when we respect and appreciate the characteristic, or negative when we do not.[23] Like most stereotypes, the statements above fail to provide a true picture of what it means to be a citizen of a particular country. Would you agree, for example, with the characterization of Americans as loving "steaks and big cars"? How about an alternative description of all Americans as "young, rich, and famous"? Does this seem accurate to you? Why or why not? Can you articulate reasons why this stereotype could have emerged in global culture?

Second, different group cultures can often be identified inside existing country borders. Beyond the 200 independent countries, there are literally thousands of distinct national identities. State political boundaries often convey a misleading impression that all people who live within those boundaries think of themselves first and foremost as "French" or "Chinese" or "American." In fact the international system is riddled with thousands of distinct identities that might best be characterized as ethnic national or indigenous groups. These groups may share demographic characteristics such as language, race, and religion, or less measurable characteristics such as common historical experience, regular social interaction, or common values and beliefs. Ultimately, these groups share a perceptual sense of community. The study of different national and identity group cultures (and subcultures) is a fascinating enterprise, as any anthropologist will attest.

In preparing to study abroad, you might also think about how identity group differences may be more distinct in your host country. In some cases, you will land in a foreign country where there is a fairly homogenous cultural and national identity (e.g., Japan or the Scandinavian countries). You are much more likely, though, to end up in a country where there are palpable identity group differences. In these countries there may be examples of discrimination by one identity group over another and sometimes limited political rights for certain minorities. One may discover these differences in countries all over the world, from Oman to South Africa, from Argentina to Australia. You might look out for disparities between rich and poor, majorities and minorities, certain racial or ethnic groups, university students and governments, or men and women in the host culture.

It often comes as a surprise just how significant ethnic national differences are for politics in your country of study. Catalan nationalism in Spain and Quebecois independence drives in Canada have threatened federal unity in those countries for decades, for example, and you might see some signs of these dynamics at work when you study abroad. In some African, European, and Asian countries you will learn about ethnic identity differences that have characterized economic and political divides for hundreds of years. At their most extreme, identity group conflicts have broken out in full-fledged wars between and inside states. While you are highly unlikely to study in a country with political violence, there may still be a legacy of identity conflict to learn more about through study or even fieldwork.

Group identity is important, but ultimately culture is manifest at the individual level. Here again we emphasize that traditional stereotypes of national culture or even identity groups do not necessarily define individuals. You will find that, just as in the United States, every person with whom you interact is different. Not all Irish youth enjoy going to the pub. Some Belgians support a socialist government while others prefer U.S.-style capitalism. For better or worse, Aboriginal groups in Australia do not all pursue the same agenda in their activism toward the national government. Thus, the best response to cultural differences at the national, local, or individual level is to respectfully plunge right in. And we urge you to do just this—interact with as many individuals as possible, from your friends and peers in class to the local butcher to your mates on sports teams. The ability to see individuals as different from common stereotypes and generalizations is, in fact, a skill in cross-cultural literacy.[24] This is also a great way to learn about and experience culture in all its fascinating dimensions.

Experiential Learning and Vocational Development

Your plan for study abroad represents both a powerful tradition in higher education and a new trend toward experiential learning. There is ample

Lauren Merriman, Wooster in Chiang Mai, Thailand

scholarly literature that shows how we can learn a great deal about things by actually participating in our own education. A famous teacher-scholar, John Dewey, began to study and write about the value of experiential learning more than 100 years ago. He argued that firsthand experience creates a deeper level of understanding and can greatly enhance traditional education.[25] Today, active teaching and learning approaches recognize the value of meaningful student engagement in the discovery of knowledge. Collaboration between students and instructors can be empowering and inspiring for new research and exploration of significant questions.[26]

The contemporary active teaching and learning literature shows that techniques that engage students in collaborative learning practices can help achieve key educational objectives, including promoting a deeper understanding of the concepts, allowing students to make conceptual linkages between theory and real-world examples, and increasing retention of knowledge.[27] Experiential learning helps enrich student understanding of key concepts by framing them through their own life experiences. Studies show that students retain far less information when they simply read or hear lectures versus having a personal experience, from conducting fieldwork to giving class presentations.[28]

Some study abroad programs around the world have been structured on the model of experiential learning espoused by Dewey and his supporters. For example, there is a strong emphasis on experiential education in service of social justice at Augsburg College's Center for Global Education. The center offers semester-long and short-term programs and travel seminars focused on innovative themes such as women in health care and agriculture in Cuba and sustainable development in Guatemala and El Salvador.[29] The University of Minnesota sponsors programs focused on ethics and social justice all around the world. As a further example, various programs led by U.S. universities in India support intensive language study of Hindi, arts and culture seminars, and classes on instrumental and vocal music and religious traditions including Hinduism, Buddhism, Islam, Sikhism, and Jainism.

Field study can be a powerful experiential component of study abroad programs, and hundreds of programs around the world feature hands-on learning opportunities for vocational development. For instance, the School for International Training (SIT), the higher education institute of the third-party education provider World Learning, is a leader in this field. For decades, SIT has specialized in offering unique combinations of programs that blend traditional classroom instruction with homestays, language immersion, and intensive field study experiences. Students may learn firsthand about ecological problems in the Amazon basin rainforest of Brazil, societal challenges in Lesotho, economic development problems in the Ashanti region of Ghana, the impact of development and revival of Islam in Jordan, or the effects of global economic changes on Mongolia's nomads. As another example, students who participate in the School for Field Studies Wildlife Management program in Kenya receive intensive training and skills in mapping or surveying human or animal impact by participating in hands-on research in Kenyan national parks. Students enrolled at the Australian National University may intern with Members of Parliament in Canberra, Australia, gaining direct experience with national political dynamics in a foreign country.

More and more educational programs also incorporate some dimension of service learning. This is experiential learning designed to provide a needed service to the community while allowing students to learn and apply course concepts in the real world.[30] It differs from community service in that the former involves the interdependent linkages between coursework and volunteer activity. Thus, coursework is informed by student action, and action is informed by, and occurs within the context of, the academic study of relevant topics. Studies show that the most successful active learning exercises are those that are linked directly to classes, carefully interwoven into the learning process set out in any academic program.[31]

Study abroad can also help you learn about topics in disciplines ranging from comparative literature, culture, politics, and the arts to science, language, and religion. Some disciplines have highly specific skill sets that can be attained through study abroad. Foreign language immersion and training are certainly foremost among these. Students who major in a language at their home institution may through overseas study achieve language fluency, an integral part of their studies. Related disciplinary training can be achieved, say, by linking Mandarin Chinese training with classes in international economics and business. Specialized foreign study programs in areas like music composition, mining and engineering, art history, anthropology, or architecture may provide students with unique skills that are considered essential for vocational training. After all, where better to study the ethnic indigenous movements of the world than in Mexico or Guatemala, where several native tribes vie for influence in relation to the national government? Where better to learn about advancements in mathematics and physics than at the same European universities where many important theorems were first devised or great scientific discoveries occurred? Where better to develop true fluency in the Russian language than by living in Yekaterinburg or Moscow for a semester or longer? Study abroad in and of itself encompasses the values and benefits of experiential learning.

Crossing Cultures and Responsible Global Citizenship

Study abroad can help promote responsible global citizenship. While scholars disagree over which exact qualities characterize a "global citizen," common themes do come through in the literature. For example, Taso Lagos has characterized global citizenship as "the purview of individuals to live, work and play within transnational norms and status that defy national boundaries and sovereignty." Global citizens are "people that can travel within these various layers or boundaries and somehow still make sense of the world."[32] Eve Stoddard and Grant Cornwell define a "citizen of the world" as someone who is "sufficiently experienced in the ways of diverse cultures that she can bracket her own frames of identity and belief enough to be comfortable with multiple perspectives, to suspend disbelief in the presence of new cultures and new ways of seeing.

[One's] own local or national identities are not held with blind commitment, but subject to evaluation and comparison with those of others."[33]

For the purposes of this project, global citizenship refers to the ability of individuals to transcend borders, both internal and personal, and external and cultural. It involves the development of sensitivity to other cultures, the ability to make reasonable cognitive and social adjustments when crossing cultures, and the desire to become an advocate for greater international understanding and cooperation. In essence, it encompasses an understanding of the interrelations among the local, national, and global, and a commitment to action within these interconnected spheres.

It is perfectly natural for us as individuals to begin our educational journey with a somewhat ethnocentric, or inwardly focused, worldview. After all, we are each a product of our cultural upbringing. Our socialization may sometimes lead to parochialism, an inwardly focused sense of superiority about one particular way of life. Optimists believe that globalization has become an engine for overcoming this parochialism through critical thinking and experiential learning. For instance, Richard Slimbach argues, "more persons than ever before are pursuing lives that link the local and the global. They are becoming increasingly transcultural."[34] In this complex new world, he believes in the capacity to demonstrate personal qualities and standards "of the heart" (e.g., empathy, inquisitiveness, initiative, flexibility, humility, sincerity, gentleness, justice, and joy) within specific intercultural contexts in which one is living and learning.[35]

Study abroad facilitates achieving greater levels of "intercultural competence" or sensitivity. As defined by Milton Bennett, these skills refer to "the ability to think and act in interculturally appropriate ways."[36] Intercultural sensitivity is an even higher level of cross-cultural understanding wherein individuals are "increasingly capable of accommodating cultural difference" in an altered worldview.[37] This theme is discussed in greater depth in Chapter 4. Globally competent citizens, comfortable in a variety of communities, are thus able to make necessary accommodations and adjustments when crossing cultures. Take, for example, the seemingly simple idea of a personal sense of space. When one of our colleagues opened her umbrella during a downpour in India recently, hordes of people rushed under it with her to keep dry. Riding the Tube in London or a bus in Seoul, South Korea, will also challenge your American sense of space rather quickly. Whatever your background, it is important to be prepared to be surprised. And preparing for cross-cultural exchange through careful research and forethought can make a vast difference in how one manages these cross-cultural encounters that will result in developed intercultural sensitivity and learning.[38]

Higher levels of intercultural competence can thus lead students to a more defined notion of global citizenship through "learning to assume responsibility for one's own citizen commitments while appreciating and developing the ability to respectfully represent differences of other nations, communities and worldviews."[39] By navigating comfortably through various levels of "citizenship" and "community," students become more aware of their roles as responsible citizens of the world.

Ultimately, what really matters is how we deal with the challenges of facing the world as globally competent and responsible citizens. Experts agree that crossing cultures and engaging in new and different communities can be a profound experience, and that study abroad needs to be envisioned as a deeper component of educational development and curriculums. Institutions are developing more study abroad predeparture programs and study abroad classes. You may even be reading this book as an assignment in such a class. Put another way, there is a movement afoot—one that will help you better prepare for the adjustments and accommodations you will inevitably need to make in cross-cultural education. This is also likely to promote a more holistic impression of your experience.

There is little doubt that overseas study can promote deeper understanding of contending themes such as gender, race, ethnicity, and cultural understanding, but the experience also sets a critical foundation for lifelong learning about different cultures and societies.[40] As former secretary of state Colin Powell said:

> The more we know about each other, the more we learn about each other, the more we engage in our differences that we have between our societies and between our social systems and between our political points of view, the better off we are. The more dialogue we have at every level and especially at the academic level, where opinion-makers are located . . . the better off we are. The more we . . . understand each other, the more effective we will be in creating a world of global citizens, and the better our chances of achieving peace in our increasingly interdependent world.[41]

Empowering global citizens may thus become a means to a much greater end.

Overview of the Book

The chapters that follow take the reader on an educational journey, offering guidance and academic rationales for important decisions along the way. They are targeted at you, the student preparing for study abroad. They also address important considerations for faculty members advising the process and even families that support you on your journey.

Chapter 2 addresses how to choose the right program for your educational needs. It explores the motivations behind selection of study abroad opportunities and pathways for identifying the best programs for students. The chapter provides a clear set of typologies to categorize study abroad programs and resources and suggestions for how to obtain the best information about programs and standards.

Chapter 3 outlines additional steps to adequately prepare for study abroad experiences. You will need a sound academic foundation for education abroad. You should consider the most appropriate classes to help you prepare for the academic challenges you will encounter abroad. You should speak with professors and staff members who can help you prepare for an enriching study abroad program. Indeed, mentors play an important role in aiding student integration of the study abroad experience into an individualized program of study. Finally, this chapter discusses how you can prepare yourself and your family for immersion in a cross-cultural learning experience.

Chapter 4 focuses on meaningful participation in study abroad. First, we introduce models for thinking about what culture really means and encourage participants to begin to explore intercultural sensitivity. The chapter then outlines practical steps that any participant in foreign study can take to experience a truly transformative immersion experience. The chapter explores some extremely important themes that you might typically encounter, such as issues of psychological and social adaptation. Ultimately, the steps outlined in this chapter will help you transition from simply living a "parallel existence" in another place to transcultural literacy.

Chapter 5 focuses on reentry and reorientation to your home institution. We discuss the realities of the transition back home and the importance of meaningful assessment and debriefing of the experience. The chapter also introduces strategies for deeper reflection on study abroad. The chapter discusses both institutional programming to facilitate educational journeys before and after the study abroad experience and personal steps to address reentry challenges.

Chapter 6 explores how education abroad provides students not only with opportunities for critical reflection but also valuable vocational development. This chapter explores ways for you to contextualize your experiences and begin to frame your work in terms of valuable career development in a globalizing economy. This chapter is also about the continuation of the educational journey—building meaningfully on your experience through college work and potential international careers, internships, or even graduate school abroad.

Finally, the Worksheets section features several worksheets for predeparture orientation and reentry reflection framed in an academic context. The Resources provide up-to-date information about academic preparation for cross-cultural experiences. The material builds on our model of the global classroom as a journey framed around a core of academic development. Included are references to a number of contemporary online and print resources. Additional information for easy use by students, parents, faculty members, and practitioners is also included.

Chapter Two
HOW TO CHOOSE THE RIGHT
PROGRAM FOR YOU

To get the most out of your study abroad experience, it is time to investigate the different options available and reflect on how your program choice matches your personal and academic goals. In this chapter we provide food for thought on program location, model, length, and options for learning experiences. We also provide some practical tips for obtaining the information you need (see Figure 2.1).

Figure 2.1 The Global Classroom Learning Cycle

Program Paradigms

It is natural to feel overwhelmed at first by both the world of opportunities before you and also the new terminology you are likely to encounter. There are literally thousands of different programs out there. When we talk about study abroad or education abroad programs, we refer to credit-bearing activities, either inside or outside the classroom, in a foreign environment.[1] As you look through the various programs available, you will encounter several terms and program models in relation to the sponsoring or organizing party. It is important to understand the following program types to know how yours will be managed.

Direct Enrollment

Students can apply directly to a foreign or "host" institution. As opposed to the home institution, the host institution is the foreign university or other unit that provides academic and programmatic support to the student. In direct enrollment programs, students may need to do much of the legwork themselves, from finding housing to registering for classes. While the "home" school, or the college or university that the student is attending, usually provides less support, students should nonetheless talk with the appropriate departments and offices on campus to be sure that credits transfer. Students should also thoroughly research the procedures for taking a leave of absence from the home school, if necessary. This option, while possibly the least expensive, requires a high level of responsibility and independence from the student.

Institutionally Run Programs

The home school may run some of its own programs. These "institutionally owned" or "homegrown" programs are organized and administered by the home institution. The home school will handle the application and registration process; conduct pre- and postprogram informational sessions; choose or create courses; manage living arrangements, activities, and excursions; and usually provide extensive service and logistical organization for students. There is often at least one representative from your school or faculty member on-site who will oversee the program. Usually, the application and credit transfer processes are simplified, but costs may be marginally higher than for other programs.

Institution-Sponsored Exchanges

Direct exchange, or "seat-for-seat," programs allow students to directly enroll in a foreign university while a student from that university attends the home school. Similar to institutionally run programs, the home school organizes these exchanges through agreements with foreign institutions. Like direct enrollment, this type of program may involve a great deal of independence and research on the part of the student.

Program Providers or Third-Party Programs

Many colleges and universities contract with third-party program providers. These organizations have various levels of affiliations with the home school, but the programs are not run by the home institution. The third-party provider might be an institutional unit of a college or university, such as programs run by Antioch Education Abroad or by Arcadia University's Center for Education Abroad. They might also be run by a nonprofit group, like IES Abroad, or even for-profit organizations. The outside organization may or may not have a "school of record," or an affiliation with an accredited institution of higher education in the United States that grants credit for courses taken abroad. Students should check with their home institution to know if a school of record is required, or if credit is accepted directly from the program provider. The third-party organization takes care of admission to the foreign institution, housing, orientation, and in most cases provides on-site staff and other services. Although often a more expensive option, these programs offer a high degree of service and provide culturally integrated activities.

Program Characteristics

Students, faculty, and family members are sometimes surprised to learn that not all study abroad programs are created equal: distinct elements set each program apart. With that in mind, Lilli Engle and John Engle provide a classification of program type based on combinations of seven defining characteristics.[2] Their classification is founded in intercultural theory and research illustrating that a student's learning experience can be affected by these program characteristics, and that certain program elements encourage cultural learning and development to varying degrees. It goes without saying that a thematically focused six-week program where students live in a hostel and all classes are conducted in English is a very different experience from that of a yearlong program where students live with host families and are fully integrated into a local university. Engle and Engle offer the following program characteristics to consider:

1. *Program length:* Does the program last for a semester, a full year, or is it a short-term program (under eight weeks)?
2. *Participants' language background:* Is the program aimed at non-speakers, beginning, intermediate, or advanced-level students of a particular foreign language?
3. *Language used in coursework:* Are all, some, or no courses taught in a foreign language?
4. *Context of academic work:* Are students directly enrolled and integrated in a host university? Are courses taught by faculty from students' home institution? Are classes taught by host faculty but for participating students only? Or are students able to combine these models?
5. *Housing:* Do students have the choice to live in apartments, participate in homestays, or stay in residence halls? Do they live alone, or with other U.S. students, international students, or local students?
6. *Learning paradigms:* Are there opportunities for structured cultural or experiential learning? Does the program offer study in a local university, internships, volunteering for academic credit, field study, focused language training, or general university training? Is it localized in a single location or is it a traveling program? Are courses taught by one professor or are they team taught?
7. *Cultural learning:* Is there on-site guided reflection on the cultural learning experience? Is there on-site or post-experience orientation and reentry programming, advising, cross-cultural work integrated into courses, or individualized cultural research projects?

Engle and Engle emphasize that students consider the "compatibility of program components" in relation to their academic and personal goals. For example, if a student's schedule only allows summer study and the academic goal is to learn about a specific theme in a precise culture—

Dana Bustamante, SIT Study Abroad, Kenya

to learn about traditional African music, for example—then perhaps a study tour or a short-term program might work best. But if a German major's academic goal is to become fluent in the language, then a cross-cultural immersion program where all classes are conducted in that language and the student attends the local university might be the best option for academic growth.

The importance of program types can be illustrated in research conducted on three different short-term study abroad programs in Cuba. One program was a type of "study tour," or add-on to a university course taken at the U.S. home institution. Most likely due to the structure provided by the on-campus course, students demonstrated preprogram expectations closely matching perceived challenges after the end of the program. For the program that offered the most contact with locals from a cross section of the Cuban culture, students showed greater perceived challenges of language learning and understanding and adapting to the culture and lifestyle of the country.[3] For example, living with a host family was a challenging learning experience for the students. Since programs offer various developmental outcomes, it is important to consider models and elements carefully as you begin to plan your study abroad experience.

Academic Opportunities

Think about your academic goals for studying abroad and how a program's design and focus can complement those goals. Different programs often feature different academic or experiential learning opportunities—from the languages spoken to methods of learning to classroom atmosphere—that might correspond to your objectives for studying abroad.

It is no surprise that learning a foreign language is a very common goal in study abroad, and surely living in a different country is the best way to become fluent in another language. But we encourage you to think carefully about your language learning goals. Do you seek introductory training or more profound proficiency in a foreign language? What are your goals for developing listening, reading, writing, and speaking proficiency? What are your long-term career goals, and how will language training enhance your profile on the job market someday? In addition, remember that foreign language learning is an important step in personal development and, ultimately, one's quest for intercultural competence. Learning a language, being pushed outside of your comfort zone, struggling to communicate: these experiences force you to reconsider the world around you.[4]

If you seek proficiency in Mandarin, you will likely consider studying in China. If you want to cultivate your Spanish skills, you might think about the pros and cons of studying in Latin America versus Spain. But even within these countries or regions, there are related items to consider. For example, natives in Barcelona speak Catalan and not the Spanish you might be familiar with from your classes. The dialects and vocabulary in Latin America differ from those in Spain. And of course, languages are not limited to those spoken in Western Europe. Professionals see increasing interest in less commonly taught or "nontraditional" languages and destinations. Since 1965, enrollment in Arabic classes has grown 300 percent, 475 percent in Chinese, and 875 percent in Japanese, while the growth in traditional languages is less staggering with 64 percent for Spanish, and declines in French and German.[5] Furthermore, as economies of nontraditional locations grow and gain political importance in global politics, learning about these countries and cultures is a means to better understanding of geopolitics and the world economy.

Academic options are not limited to foreign language learning. More study abroad programs are embedding experiential learning elements, such as internships, volunteering, or field research, within their programs. Internships and service learning come in a variety of formats—some quite different from what you might expect in the United States. And because these are popular active learning options, many programs offer extensive opportunities. Internships can range from an English-teaching assistantship to working in a marketing firm or serving as a staff assistant in the Parliament of Scotland. Service learning might include working at a soup kitchen, playing with children in an after-school program, or helping at a local clinic.

Besides requiring heavy time commitments, experiential activities like these can be challenging. As you work closely with locals to complete tasks or if local agencies are understaffed and struggle to work with minimal resources, you could feel frustrated. That said, as they are forced to leave the comfort zone of the traditional classroom, participants in experiential activities also report significant changes in their outlooks about the host country and their home country, as well as immense personal growth and language and cultural learning. The service learning component adds an additional opportunity and context for interaction that fosters "an ecology of active learning."[6]

Field research is another unique method of gaining cross-cultural disciplinary experience. Besides providing the opportunity for subject-specific learning and working closely with a professional in your field, intensive research during study abroad can offer other benefits linked to intercultural learning, from language to cross-cultural communication skills. As described by study abroad professionals Mel Bolen and Patricia Martin:

> Developing research skills in an international context means that students must learn how to navigate in another culture. Students must interact with people who are not their peers and who are outside a traditional classroom setting. By approaching organizations and individuals that inform their research, students learn much about the workings of the culture. And success in one attempt to navigate a host culture can lead to success in further attempts. For the student-researcher, persistence is necessary because their research goal depends on successfully gaining access to the information they require. Cross-cultural skills are the tools that enable student-researchers to accomplish their goals and finish their projects.[7]

The skills learned during field research abroad, in conjunction with interactions with the host culture, will allow you to advance academically and personally during your experience.

Learning can occur in venues other than the credit-bearing portion of the program. Experiential activities such as field trips, site visits, cultural activities, social activities, tandem language programs, conversation clubs, or weekend trips open up opportunities for engaging with the culture. They provide you with experiences that you might not find on your own, such as spending a day at the local parliament to learn about how the government works, or visiting a bakery to learn about how the local bread is made. Likewise, social activities, such as weekly conversation groups or language partner programs, make socializing and meeting peers easier at the same time you are learning the language. Such activities, when well integrated into the learning environment and program structure, and surrounded by structured preparation and debriefing, are invaluable learning experiences. Underlining the importance of program organization, research shows, a well-structured overall learning environment encourages the development of intercultural competencies.[8] These extracurricular program elements are equally important to consider as you explore your options for learning and growth.

Other Program Considerations

Program Length and Timing

Program length and timing deserve special consideration. Students now have a wealth of choices, such as study abroad for a full year, a semester, a shorter summer term, a "January term," or "May-mester," or even for a few days or weeks on a program "embedded" in a class at the home school. Of the 241,791 students abroad sent from U.S. institutions of higher education in 2006–2007, 55.4 percent of them went on short-term programs (eight weeks or less), 40.2 percent on mid-length programs (one semester, one quarter, or two quarters), and 4.4 percent on long-term programs (one academic or calendar year).[9] When deciding on the length of time that you will study abroad, take into consideration your home institution's policies in addition to wider personal and academic variables.

In addition to the program and home institution requirements, you may have personal circumstances that can affect choice of program duration and timing. As an example, consider the situation of students with health or disability concerns. A study done at Landmark College shows that the novelty and intensity of shorter programs, for example, were more suitable for students with learning disabilities or Attention Deficit Hyperactivity Disorder, given that these students tend to show difficulty in sustaining attention for longer periods of time. Students were able to remain attentive and interested in shorter programs, with more intense and directed academic focus on one or two courses, and without the concerns of other extracurricular distractions.[10] It is each student's responsibility to consider individual situations and goals in choosing a program model that will allow for the most personal growth and development.

Research shows that personal growth, intercultural awareness, academic performance, language learning, and vocational development can occur on a program of any length. What matters most is how you prepare for and engage in the program, taking advantage of all opportunities for learning and growth. Studying abroad for a full year allows you greater opportunity for a variety of interactions with local citizens and culture—from taking more university courses to living with a host family, elements that are more challenging to accomplish on shorter-term programs. In turn, this often promotes greater intercultural awareness and the development of a more sophisticated worldview.[11] However, you can also gain cultural awareness, vocational training, and personal growth on shorter-term programs. For example, one study shows that students on a two-week trip to Guatemala and Belize took advantage of the structured opportunities provided by the program to quickly develop coping strategies and teamwork skills. The intimacy of the group dynamics most likely played an important role.[12] In a well-structured format allowing for reflection, short-term programs can offer significant growth and learning experiences.[13]

The moment in your academic career at which you choose to study abroad can also play a role in how you process the experience, and your choices are increasing. Most students study abroad during their junior or senior year: in 2006–2007, 36.6 percent of students studying abroad were college juniors and 21.3 percent were seniors. The remainder consisted of other undergraduate and graduate students. However, over the past ten years, the percentage of freshman undergraduates studying abroad has grown from 2.4 percent to 3.3 percent of all students abroad.[14] Because juniors have a firmer idea of their academic interests and goals while freshman- and sophomore-level students are still exploring academic options, the third year is often chosen as the appropriate moment for study abroad. In addition, students might wish to reserve the senior year for completing graduation requirements at their home school. In any case, timing your program can play a role in how you are able to process and reflect on it in regard to your larger academic plans.

Living Arrangements

Living arrangements are an especially important element in your choice of program. Be sure to research what sort of housing options are available in relation to your personal needs and desires as well as the potential for learning afforded by available accommodations. Your program might offer independent housing in private apartments, student housing in a university residence hall, or a homestay arrangement. Some programs only offer one option; others offer several different opportunities. Within these configurations, roommate or family selection, meals, bathroom arrangements, kitchen privileges, and laundry and Internet access vary widely, as do your level of independence and opportunities for cultural integration and language learning.

Living with a local family in a homestay arrangement is ideal for language and cultural immersion. Students tend to find it easier to assimilate into the culture through full-immersion living arrangements. At the same time, a successful homestay experience requires negotiation and a bit of risk: you have less independence than you might be used to, and you are bound to run up against linguistic and cultural barriers that will require you to be flexible and open-minded. You must familiarize yourself with expectations and rules in regard to your hosts or roommates. In choosing a full-immersion housing experience, consider the level of interaction that would make you feel the most comfortable while allowing you to best benefit and grow during your experience. Would you feel more at ease around an older couple or a young family with children? Do you want to be treated as a member of the host family, as a guest, or as a friend?

While living with fellow U.S. students may seem like the easiest option, it often becomes far more challenging to learn about your host culture and make local friends. Students often find it beneficial to have foreign or host country roommates to ease the integration process and enrich cultural and language learning. One study compared language learning in U.S. students abroad in Spain with that of students attending Spanish courses at their home institution in the United States. The study found that the more students communicated regularly with native

speakers, the less they had to resort to "tricks" to fill in information gaps in conversation. Using the language in context allowed students to become more aware of the practical aspects of communication.[15] The opportunity to speak with locals twenty-four hours a day, seven days a week, will surely help you to improve your language proficiency. No matter which living situation you choose, be aware of the benefits and challenges associated with it.

Location

This is where many students begin their exploration of program options, and it goes without saying that your destination of study can influence the educational experience. The trend for many decades of study abroad has been for students to travel to Western European destinations. Today, the United Kingdom and other European countries still remain the most popular study abroad destinations. The United Kingdom hosts 14.6 percent of all study abroad participants, Italy 12.5 percent, Spain 10.7 percent, and France 7.7 percent.[16] It is worth noting, though, that the number of study abroad students in Europe is growing at a much slower pace than at many nontraditional locations.

More and more programs are being offered in nontraditional locations in developing countries such as India or Argentina. Indeed, these programs are increasing in popularity so rapidly that referring to them as "nontraditional" seems passé: China now hosts 4.9 percent of all students and Argentina 1.6 percent. While we are by no means anti-Europe in our orientation toward study abroad, we would encourage you to think creatively about your destination and program. Instead of studying in London, England, for example, consider Chennai, India; instead of Madrid, Spain, think about Quito, Ecuador. There are incredible educational advantages to such a choice. As Megan Che, Mindy Spearman, and Agida Manizade argue:

> Study abroad programs targeting less familiar destinations have a potential for student development, social good, and for increasing cultural awareness and global mindedness to a greater degree than those that target more familiar locations. This is because the more rich opportunities to experience struggle and cognitive dissonance while simultaneously interacting with more capable others contribute to a higher likelihood of the construction of an authentic, deep space or zone for development and transformation.[17]

Thus, choosing a location with which you are less familiar may allow you to reach outside of your defined, bordered comfort zone and gain greater global awareness. Given the ever-increasing choice of programs available, Worksheet 2: "Selecting the Right Program for You" (featured in the Worksheets section) offers useful ways to frame your decision on academic goals, program focus, location, and classes.

How to Get the Information You Need

It is easy to feel lost as you research the best study abroad program for your needs and goals, but a number of resources are available to help you. First, consult your institution's study abroad office and your faculty adviser. If your school has a list of endorsed or approved programs, start with this list and browse the individual program websites. Ask the study abroad office at your school if there is an off-campus study fair, and attend it. Such an event is an ideal opportunity to ask questions of representatives from the programs, pick up brochures, and get a general, overall view of program options. If your school does not have a list of approved programs, consider the issues outlined in this chapter in relation to your goals and to your home institution's policies and procedures while you browse study abroad programs on the Internet.[18] A safe program of high academic quality is essential to an enriching and beneficial study abroad experience.

A good method for choosing a program is to narrow down the immense range of options to a more defined list that you can research in depth. You might approach this in a similar way to how you conducted your college search. Don't be afraid to ask the programs for brochures or for past program reviews or evaluations. A good program will provide you with a contact person who will truthfully and efficiently answer all of your questions. Practical questions might include the following:

Academics

- Where do classes take place? Can I take classes at the local university?
- Who will my classmates be? International students? Local students? Other U.S. students?

- What are the prerequisites to attend the program?
- Am I required to take a language course in the program?
- Is there any assistance for choosing classes? For registering at the local university?
- How many credits will I get for one course? How about for internships, field research, or service learning?
- Who teaches the courses? Local or U.S. faculty?
- If I need tutoring, how can I obtain it?

Predeparture Services

- How does the program prepare me for my experience abroad?
- Will the program assist me in obtaining a student visa, if necessary?

On-Site Services

- What type of in-country orientation is provided?
- What sorts of activities exist to help me integrate into the host culture and meet local peers? Are field trips available and included in program cost?
- What sort of on-site support staff is available?
- What are the housing options? How do you select housing for students?

Safety and Security

- Is there a code of disciplinary and academic conduct?
- Does the program require additional study abroad health insurance? What does it cover? If I get sick or need medical help while abroad, how will you assist me?
- What happens if there is an emergency or crisis situation while I am on-site?

Costs

- What is the total program cost and what does it cover?
- Can my financial aid transfer?
- Do you provide any need- or merit-based scholarships?

The questions above reflect the issues covered in this chapter and the standards outlined in industry guidelines. Often, your college or university will have already vetted programs for you based on their own well-defined criteria, but you might also base your research on published program standards, such as the Forum on Education Abroad's *Standards of Good Practice*.[19] These guidelines consider several elements of the study abroad experience in analyzing program quality: learning environment and opportunities, intercultural and communication development, academic support resources, program administration, predeparture support, on-site services, ethical policies and procedures, and student health and safety. Guidelines such as these provide a framework and set of standards for evaluating programs.

Let's take program structure as an example of how these guidelines can help you. The program should provide structured elements in the student learning experience, from predeparture and on-site cultural and academic orientation to on-site advising and a well-designed curriculum taught by engaged and qualified faculty. It should take advantage of, and encourage you to take advantage of, the local environment and provide integrated language learning opportunities when appropriate. This might include social and cultural activities, field study, or excursions. Published guidelines will help you identify the important aspects that make up a high-quality study abroad program.

Program costs and finances are important considerations as well. After discussing program cost with your study abroad adviser or the program representative, make a list of possible expenditures and find out who covers these expenses. A summary list of expenses might consist of the following:

- Tuition
- Housing
- Room, board, utilities
- Health insurance
- Books
- Airfare
- In-country travel
- Daily transport
- Passport and visa fees and photographs
- Excursions (field trips, travel, and cultural events either with your program or individually)

- Personal expenses (postcards, postage, household items, laundry, clothing, entertainment, local cell phone, Internet access, and long-distance communication)

A similar list will help formulate a clearer idea of the cost of study abroad for you and your family, but it should also be compared to other program elements and their priority to you. As you analyze programs, be sure to compare "apples to apples"—have a clear idea of what the programs offer and require of you in order to compare them fairly. Then, discuss the program with your study abroad adviser and your institution's financial aid and business offices to determine how the billing for the program is conducted and if your financial aid will transfer.

In addition to the study abroad staff at your school and program representatives, returnees who have attended these programs in the past can serve as helpful and interesting sources of firsthand information. Their opinions and reports, both positive and negative, will provide details on how the program functions as well as its highlights, strengths, and weaknesses. Likewise, international students from the country where you would like to study might enlighten you as to customs, traditions, climate, student life, or academics in their home countries. Keep in mind that personal accounts are just that—highly personal—and you must base your decision on your own evaluations.

Considerations for Students with Special Needs

Careful consideration and research are necessary for students with disabilities and special needs. Although U.S. laws recognize specific conditions as disabilities, not all countries have the same regulations and viewpoints, and this may affect program choice and your experience abroad. Do you prefer a program that can easily accommodate your disability, or is the specific destination more important than accommodations? How does the program structure fit your learning needs? How will the program's medical insurance affect you? When you have defined your goals and chosen a handful of possible programs, communicate with the program and your study abroad adviser to best identify your needs. Disclosing your disability early on in the application process facilitates accommodation. A number of associations in the United States and abroad can assist you in disclosure as well as accommodation while on site.[20] It is important to be realistic about the challenges that a program might present and to remember that many people with disabilities have traveled and studied abroad successfully and benefited immensely from the experience.

Conclusion

Clearly there is a lot to consider when making an informed choice about study abroad. In this chapter we have reviewed ways that you can familiarize yourself with the options available to you in relation to your school's policies on study abroad and requirements for graduation. We have also emphasized the importance of thinking about program elements in connection with the dimensions of learning noted in Chapter 1: culture, identity, vocational training, and global citizenship. Don't hesitate to speak with family and friends to best formulate your goals and discuss program options. But always keep in mind that, like your choice of major or which elective course to take, the decision to study abroad, and in which program, is your own.

Choosing the program that is the best fit for you is a key step to ensuring a meaningful, beneficial learning experience abroad. Be sure to take the time necessary to ask yourself questions about the program and think about the many factors involved, from the practical aspects of program duration, location, model, or requirements, to your academic and personal goals, your desires, and your specific needs. The task of selecting a study abroad program should not be taken lightly, as it is the key to a memorable, challenging, and rewarding experience.

Chapter Three
ALMOST THERE:
PREPARING TO STUDY ABROAD

Choosing the appropriate program is an important step, but preparing for a meaningful study abroad experience does not end there. You also need a sound academic foundation to maximize your experience, as well as an understanding of your own cultural and personal identity and what you want to get out of the experience. You can begin your preparation by enrolling in appropriate classes before you leave and engaging thoughtfully in predeparture orientation programs. Furthermore, you will want to do some independent research on your host culture, ways to communicate with home, and how to ensure your health and safety while overseas. These measures will help you and your family to prepare for a meaningful experience that will maximize your educational and personal goals.

Academic Objectives

The study abroad experience should be viewed as a holistic educational journey, clearly linked to your academic goals (see Figure 3.1). The academic preparation and skill-building for study abroad discussed in this chapter are a natural progression of the goal formulation and program choice that you have worked on thus far. Although your time abroad is bound to be a life-changing experience, remember that you are preparing for *study* abroad: the academic component should be central to your plans.

Figure 3.1 The Global Classroom Learning Cycle

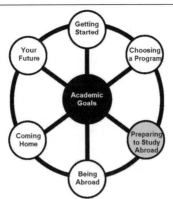

You can lay the groundwork for a successful experience by taking classes now that provide a foundation for what you plan to do abroad. For example, you might prepare for an internship or field research by taking courses that will complement experiential learning opportunities (e.g., the proper science courses for an internship in a laboratory, or economics courses to prepare you for work with a multinational corporation). If you plan on volunteering as an English teaching assistant, consider enrolling in a pedagogical theory course before you go. Moreover, if you intend to take classes at a foreign university, remember that the academic systems in other countries are often quite different from that of the United States. For example, in many European universities, upper-level courses treat material in a manner far more specific than in the United States. Instead of a course on seventeenth-century French literature, an entire semester-long course might analyze a single work by Montaigne. You can prepare for these differences by talking to your professors in advance and by taking in-depth, upper-level classes before you go.

Remember to research the prerequisites for work on your program. For example, if you were hoping to take a biochemistry course at your host university you might need a specific background in biology and chemistry. If you are a studio art major in the United States and have been accepted to a program that allows you to take courses at a prestigious fine arts school abroad, be sure that you have a good foundation of similar coursework at your own institution.

For students planning to study in a country where English is not the native language, one of the most important ways to prepare for your time abroad is through language learning. Besides the very practical benefits of increasing the variety of courses available to you on-site, efforts to speak the local language from the moment you arrive in your host country show your desire and ability to understand and fit in with the local culture. You will find that as your ease of communication increases, potentially negative cultural interactions and culture shock will decrease. As an example, a study done by the American University Center of Provence shows that students who have already had two years of a foreign language before beginning the program abroad (a common prerequisite for full-immersion language programs) exhibit significant development in openness and intercultural sensitivity.[1] The ability to participate in the classroom and in conversations with peers will not only make your integration and adaptation quicker and easier, it will boost your self-confidence and ability to function in the foreign environment.

You can begin to prepare yourself linguistically by increasing your contact with the foreign language by watching television online and movies from the country; listening to the radio online; reading newspapers, magazines, and books; or speaking with international students or professors. Practice speaking, listening, and writing in all types of situations and on all types of topics: talk about new movies and music with international students on your home campus, write a letter to your host family to introduce yourself. Start making flash cards or jotting down new words in a journal that you can continue to use abroad.[2] Preparation through increased exposure to different languages, dialects, and accents will carry over to your study abroad experience and help you develop your intercultural communication skills.

Finally, an alternative approach is to plan to take classes abroad that are not offered at your home institution—a museology class for an art history major or an African philosophy class for a philosophy major. Indeed, education abroad can be framed as a special opportunity to take classes very different from those back home. Do not be afraid to think outside the box: engineering students might take advantage of business courses, or urban studies majors might take geography or sociology courses abroad. While often fulfilling general education and other graduation requirements, a creative combination of classes may even complement your major and render your experience more attractive on your resumé or graduate school applications.

Cross-Cultural Communication

Learning the language of your host country is very important, but that learning process extends far beyond the classroom. Language and communication are vital for cultural learning and a holistic experience in many foreign cultures. As anthropologist and cross-cultural researcher Edward T. Hall reminds us, "Culture is communication and communication is culture."[3] They are intrinsically linked. So being able to successfully communicate in another culture—both verbally and nonverbally—is essential.

Also, remember that communication is multifaceted, incorporating both words and behaviors, styles of communication, and value differences. True communication includes the slang that you never learned in your French textbook, the way a person responds to you, tone of voice and volume, or the distance two people stand from each other while talking. It can encompass when and how often you compliment the person you are speaking with, or if and how you should negotiate prices at the local market. Cultural differences affect when someone arrives at a meeting, when you should arrive for an invited dinner, and what you should bring your host as a gift. Smiling or waving hello to a citizen of Ecuador or Thailand may not have the same significance as it does to a fellow American. Thus, although language learning might begin in the classroom, learning to communicate effectively across cultures often takes place in less formal venues, from talking with international students or language teaching assistants, to listening to the radio or watching television online or reading a popular magazine from your country of study.

When you communicate within another culture, no matter what the language, your ideas of what is cultural, what is universal, and what is inherent will be challenged. When you communicate interculturally you engage within a multifaceted and diverse environment where communication is a means of reaching common goals in a climate of respect and tolerance for difference. In this environment, language is just one tool among many to represent culture: "language, thought and perception are interrelated."[4] Because communication reflects the cultural norms constructed throughout one's life, it is linked to culture and background as much as to personal characteristics.[5] It is precisely when we confront our expectations of what is culturally "normal" with new, foreign experiences that we begin to break out of our comfort zone. This is also where your journey of cultural learning and development begins.

Making Connections

Even before leaving home you will have investigated and thought carefully about your study abroad program options, the skills you want to develop, and ways to begin interacting in the new culture. Now we encourage you to learn even more about your host country and culture, and yourself, by pulling together and using some of the many easily accessible resources available to you. For example, the Internet offers an abundance of online newspapers, magazines, radio stations, blogs, travel journals, and other websites where you can learn about your country of study. Your school or local library may have a good selection of foreign books or movies. Invest in a good travel guidebook to get a general overview of the country. Attend film festivals, go to ethnic restaurants, listen to foreign radio stations online. Take advantage of the resources around you, and start drawing connections between what you learn about yourself and your culture, and what you discover about the country and culture where you plan to study abroad.

Predeparture Orientations and On-Campus Programming

The study abroad office at your college or university likely offers services to assist you in preparation for your time overseas. One of the most important of these is a predeparture orientation program. This orientation may cover topics ranging from logistical matters—health and safety, program details and schedules, administrative issues, travel and packing tips, academic issues, liability and legal matters, in-country communication, information about the host country—to matters requiring more profound reflection such as cross-cultural communication, adjustment, reentry, stereotypes, or cultural information on the host country. Orientation formats vary. You may review a handbook or PowerPoint presentation, listen to guest speakers or faculty, meet former returnees, or network with other students going abroad.[6]

Studies show that predeparture and reentry programming gives students the background and means for reflection that allow them to create a much more enriching experience from their time abroad. Orientations prepare you for a satisfying experience "by creating realistic expectations and by reducing the multitude of unknown, unpredictable factors involved in studying in a foreign country."[7] You are bound to be confronted with

some stressful situations during your overseas experience, but by simultaneously reducing some of the unknowns and discovering positive coping
mechanisms and learning methods, you will be able to better manage your
expectations and maximize the experience.

Reaching Out to Others

One of the very best ways to prepare for study abroad may be using the
human resources at your institution. As we stressed previously, continue
discussing your plans and long-term goals with your academic adviser, as
well as with the study abroad staff at your school. Many faculty members
and administrators at your institution have studied, traveled, or lived
abroad. They are usually happy to talk about their experiences. You are
bound to have friends or acquaintances that would as well. Very often,
study abroad offices have organized programs or even informal lists of
returnees that would love to share their experiences and advice with you.

You do not have to go very far to become aware of your role in our
global society: the growing number of international students on U.S.
campuses means that there are countless opportunities to learn about a
country's culture, traditions, politics, and history. Find a language partner
to practice the language of the country where you will be studying, or
merely have lunch with an international student to observe communication styles and begin understanding beliefs and values different from your
own. In doing so, you might also get a useful tip on a good restaurant in
Buenos Aires, the best way to travel through India, or how to successfully
befriend German university students. You could also consider getting
involved with activities and organizations on campus that can enhance
understanding of the host culture. For example, many universities have
international student associations and international or language houses or
dorms.

Interacting with your peers—either formally or informally—can be
a type of peer mentoring and is a useful resource for preparing to study
abroad. Some study abroad offices organize structured, peer mentoring
programs where meetings are planned and you are assigned a mentor
who is often formally trained. Otherwise, you can find peers yourself to
help you through the information-gathering process informally. A mentor can be anyone who is more experienced or advanced in a certain
area and who actively interacts and shares experiences with others.

Besides the obvious benefits of obtaining firsthand information and tips about a country, culture, or program, peer mentoring has been shown to help students develop interpersonal and communication skills, better time management, and greater self-esteem and self-efficacy, resulting in higher levels of overall satisfaction with an experience. From an academic standpoint, peer mentoring has been reported as having a positive impact on career choices, perseverance in pursuing goals, and academic achievement.[8]

In addition to the face-to-face peer mentoring and informal socializing on your campus, technology offers alternative methods of communicating with fellow students. You are familiar with podcasts, Wikis, blogs, and online social networking sites such as Facebook. These resources offer endless opportunities for gathering information on your program or networking with program alumni or fellow departing students. Online social networking is also being used by study abroad offices to create student interest groups, advertise, circulate information, or plan events. It is an ideal opportunity to learn about the program or location—anything from how credits transfer to where to find the best local restaurant—from other students, to voice your concerns and reflections while abroad, and to help others once you return. E-mail and social networking websites can facilitate openness and networking within a social group beyond everyday reach, encourage transparency, facilitate self-organization and teamwork, promote the sharing of information, and allow you to start thinking outside of your immediate environment on a grander scale.[9]

Used wisely and in a limited, responsible manner, online social networking can act as an extension of your study abroad experience. One research study completed by the University of Minnesota on the educational benefits of social networking also found that students report increased technology and communication skills, creativity, and openness to novelty and diversity through the use of social networking websites.[10] That said, remember that you are ultimately responsible for the information you put online, and that much of the information you gather online or from friends is *opinion*; so take it with a grain of salt and evaluate for yourself. Moreover, online communication can never replace the richness of face-to-face interactions.

In any case, keep in mind that many students have gone before you. Use their experience and advice, and that of study abroad professionals, professors, or international peers, as an example and lesson while you set out on your adventure. But always analyze and evaluate for yourself. This will be *your* experience and you need to make it what *you* want it to be.

What to Research

Now that you have an idea about how to start researching your program and destination, you might wonder about the type of knowledge that is important to gather. You know you need to learn about your country of study. But what questions should you ask? Think about the four dimensions of the global classroom to help you organize your questions. First, what concrete knowledge can you learn about topics like:

- Government, leaders, political parties
- Economy, trade, money, currency
- Educational system
- History
- Geography, main cities, regions, environment
- Cuisine, meals, etiquette
- Public and private transportation
- Holidays, traditions
- Media, entertainment, leisure activities, movies, television, music
- Laws, especially in relation to drugs and alcohol

To the extent possible, you should also investigate less tangible topics related to foreign cultures, such as possible stereotypes held by your hosts, attitudes toward dating and marriage, the role of women in society, disabilities, race, ethnicity, and acceptance of various world religions. Knowing about these things will help you adjust to the often challenging reactions and discussions that you might encounter.

Learning about your host country's politics and culture before your departure, as we discuss throughout this book, allows you to prepare for being an "ambassador" abroad and to begin thinking about your role as a global citizen. Think about what people might ask you and about possible topics of conversation, and research your answers ahead of time. How will you explain and discuss subjects like racial divides in the United States, America's consumer society, the lack of social welfare, foreign policy, or the presidential elections? Be able to back up and support your points of view, and be ready to understand those of your hosts.

Dana Bustamante, SIT Study Abroad, Kenya

Be sure to understand all of the practical aspects of your program in order to avoid unnecessary and sometimes negative surprises once onsite. Find out how your academic credits will transfer back to your home institution, how the courses you take abroad will count back home. Follow up with the program in regard to housing, registration, payment, and any special needs that you may have. As you research your destination, keep in mind your personal budget and expected expenses. Constant communication with your program and study abroad adviser is essential for smooth logistical functioning of your time abroad.

Finally, it is natural to feel a little overwhelmed by the logistical planning that you will encounter in your preparations. It may be helpful to think about this process much like your experience with selecting a college to attend and preparing to enroll. Be sure to read all material provided by your study abroad office and the program, and follow any checklists that they might give you. There are a multitude of print and online resources and handbooks that will also give you a good idea of how to manage practical issues such as financing study abroad, obtaining a passport and visa, managing your money, or planning for personal travel.

Managing Your Expectations: Reflecting on Identity

As you gather information, you are bound to begin formulating expectations for your experience. An expectation is how we understand and predict that a situation or event will play out. It is more than our hopes—it is our best forecast for the future based on past knowledge and experience. When you enter into a new experience, like study abroad, you bring with you the baggage and reflections from your past and your personal background that weigh on how you process the new events. These expectations are not only rational, but also emotional and affective, going from the very logical question of how you expect to be greeted by your host mother to the very value-oriented expectation of how women are treated in your host country. Perhaps you expect certain things from yourself, or from your program, or your host family. Why are expectations so important? Because we use these evaluations to guide our behavior and reactions.[11] It is important to be aware that you *do* have expectations, as instinctive and integrated into your personal value system as they may be.

Researcher Sharon Wilkinson has collected a series of common expectations students often have about study abroad. She postulates that study abroad participants generally expect to progress to a great extent in a foreign language and cultural learning and understanding, as they plan on inevitable out-of-class interaction with locals, particularly in a homestay living arrangement. They feel that, if they do not live up to these expectations, they must be deficient in some manner.[12] Wilkinson's assumptions were put to the test in a study conducted by the University of Massachusetts–Amherst on three short- and long-term programs. The study showed that participants' expectations did not always correspond to reality. Participants originally *expected* that out-of-class contacts would be the best means to enhance their language skills, but ultimately found that classroom work was equally or more beneficial to them. They did not participate in as much interaction with locals as they would have liked and did not speak as much in the foreign language as they had intended. Last, speaking and socializing with local citizens were more challenging than expected.[13]

It is easy to expound on the many gains that study abroad brings, from linguistic fluency, cultural learning, and new friendships to adventures, increased confidence, and independence. But in many instances the reality does not live up to the "dream." Ultimately, the success of your experience abroad, or at least how you perceive and evaluate your experience, will in part depend on how you deal with your academic and personal expectations in comparison to what actually occurs. When your expectations do not match reality, this can create a source of stress in the adjustment to your new environment, resulting in the "culture shock" discussed in Chapter 4.[14] If you work to understand your expectations beforehand, you will be better able to reflect on an experience that does not match up and more apt to consider yourself capable of adapting to the situation.

Take the time to reflect on potential challenges and turn your expectations about them into personal and academic goals. Goal-setting can improve both self-efficacy and actual performance. One recent study found that the very *act* of formulating goals played an important role in the development of global understanding and cross-cultural skills.[15] By talking with others, reading program materials and predeparture handbooks, attending events and meetings about study abroad, and obtaining information about your program and location of study, you will be able to formulate reasonable goals for yourself that will help you get the most out of your experience.

Managing your expectations, reflecting on your goals, and hence maximizing your learning abroad involve researching the foreign culture, anticipating difficult emotional challenges, interacting with your hosts, and pushing yourself to break out of your comfort zone. All of this requires profound reflection on *who you are*. And as we've discussed previously, learning about your personal identity allows you to gain a self-awareness that is essential to engage responsibly within your host culture.

Your Health and Safety

No matter how much you research your host country and how well you prepare, the bottom line for a successful experience is your health and safety throughout the program. This requires careful and serious predeparture planning.

Before you go, research the health and safety concerns of your country of study through websites like those of the United States Department of State and the Centers for Disease Control and Prevention. Do the same for any country where you are planning to travel while abroad. Are there special medical concerns or regional diseases in the places to which you will be traveling? Some common concerns are malaria, HIV/AIDS, hepatitis, yellow fever, tuberculosis, and illnesses linked to heat, altitude, or cold. Likewise, know which everyday supplies will be readily available, what the diet is like, how the local health system functions, how pharmacies work, and how you can obtain emergency services locally. Research your host country's medical system and facilities, and know how to get help if you should need it while on-site. Get a medical check-up either at your school's student health center or with your personal physician, and ask them any questions about health concerns. These professional medical resources should be able to provide information about recommended or required vaccinations. A multitude of resources for researching medical and safety issues are listed in the back of this book.

Alice Bauman, IES Abroad, Santiago, Chile

Even with the most careful preparation, a problem or emergency may arise. Be sure that you have proper health insurance coverage for these types of situations and that you know how to use it. Whether you manage health issues daily or consider yourself healthy, you should plan ahead to ensure good health abroad. The study abroad experience makes significant demands on your body, your mind, and your well-being. On-site program staff can help you in difficult situations, but really it is up to you to be responsible for your own health and safety.

Crisis and Emergency Response

As you prepare to study abroad, you will likely learn from your institution or program about emergency response plans. A crisis or emergency is "any significant event with potentially severe consequences that requires immediate action or response," according to the Safety Abroad First Educational Travel Information Clearinghouse, the leading resource on health and safety in study abroad.[16] Crises can be personal in nature— medical or mental health emergencies, accidents, injuries, family issues— or regional and national—natural disasters, political or civil unrest, terrorism. Some examples of crises or emergencies include physical assault, robbery, sexual assault, serious physical or emotional illness, injuries, hospitalization, terrorist attacks or threats, arrest or questioning by the police, the death of a student, and legal action involving a student.

Managing a crisis means preparing for, responding to, and recovering from the stressful situation. Crisis management starts by understanding your responsibilities in a crisis situation; knowing whom to contact, and when and how to contact them; and preparing yourself for the emotional impact of the crisis. As you think about possible crisis situations in your destination, consider the "4 S's" of your basic survival needs: safety, security, sanity, and support afterward. You might also anticipate what strategies you will use to meet those needs.[17]

Your program will do its best to ensure your health and safety, but you also have responsibilities that call upon the research and communication skills discussed previously. You should actively participate in all predeparture and on-site orientations and carefully read all of the documentation that your program provides, including information about academic and conduct policy, emergency protocol, and obtaining and using health insurance abroad. Communicate consistently both with your program and with your parents about your health and safety from the time that you apply, throughout the entire program, to the time you return home. You should also research the health and security situation in your country of study yourself, including the possible risks that you might encounter, how the health and emergency care system works, and which local laws might affect you. In general, you should take responsibility for yourself and your actions.

Students with Special Needs

Students with learning or other disabilities have been historically under-represented on study abroad programs for various reasons, from admissions criteria and misperceptions about available on-site support to cultural attitudes in other countries. It is your responsibility to learn as much about your program as you can beforehand in order to anticipate challenges and arrange for accommodations as needed. Take ownership of your disability by learning what you can do independently to accommodate your own needs. If costs are associated with accommodation, be sure to research all of your options. Many accommodations, like extra testing time or working with a tutor, are relatively simple and low cost. Take time to think of creative solutions to challenges. For example, instead of university housing, perhaps a local organization would help you find an accessible homestay. Beyond the logistical concerns, students with special challenges should be ready for cultural issues. Disability may be viewed differently in your host country, and the way disability is handled officially may not follow the same privacy rules as in the United States. You should think about doing extra research on your host country's attitudes toward your disability.

It is necessary to communicate with your school's study abroad office as well as your program both before departure and once on-site to address these issues, your concerns, and your special needs. In addition to aid provided by disability organizations in the United States and abroad, your program and study abroad office might be able to help you. Work with them to research and define accommodations and foresee daily challenges.

Mental Health Concerns

Another particular concern involves mental health. Research shows increases in psychiatric issues among college-age young adults: more and more students seek counseling, are hospitalized for mental health issues, and report taking psychotropic medications. Here are some facts about mental health issues among college-age adults in the United States:

- Eating disorders touch seven million women and one million men in the United States, and 86 percent of those suffering from an eating disorder report that the illness started before the age of 20.[18]
- Nearly 50 percent of college students report feeling so depressed at some point in time that they have trouble functioning normally, and 15 percent meet the criteria for clinical depression.[19]
- At least 25 percent of young adults will experience a depressive episode by the age of 24.[20]
- The number of students rating their emotional health as "below average" or "in the bottom 10 percent" doubled between freshman and junior year from 6 to 14 percent.[21]
- One-third of college students report that stress hinders academic performance and 15 percent report that depression or anxiety hinders academic performance.[22]

Despite the statistics, many students never disclose their problems, and this is even more of an issue for study abroad programs where the stressors of culture shock can set off deep emotional reactions that can quickly overwhelm an individual. The most important thing for students who suffer or have suffered from mental illness is to disclose this to your program well in advance. Before you leave, discuss your concerns with counselors, doctors, and study abroad staff. Learn to recognize at-risk behavior in yourself and learn healthy coping strategies for while you are abroad. Connect with past study abroad participants to better anticipate challenges. Remember that good communication is the first step in taking responsibility for yourself and for the success of your overseas experience.

Communicating with Your Family

We have pointed out the importance of communicating with others to gather information, create networks, and hence feel more comfortable about yourself and your experience. Communication is essential to your well-being and the well-being of those around you. We underlined that it is important to take responsibility for yourself and for the success of your experience. But do not neglect sharing your experience with your parents and family. Be honest and open with them. Do as much preliminary research about the program as you can and provide it to your parents or guardians. Start by sharing this book with them and directing them to resources specifically for parents provided by your institution's study abroad office, your program, or available online.[23] Keep your parents informed of your decisions and plans, give them as much information as possible about the program and its policies and procedures—especially in regard to health, safety, and emergencies—and keep in contact with them throughout the program.

As you communicate with your family about your choice to study abroad, you might run into some specific challenges. Your parents may not understand *why* you want to study abroad. Show them that it is a worthwhile endeavor. Sharing with them your reflections from the previous chapters will demonstrate that you are determined and are moving toward a definite goal. Explain to them how this experience will affect your academic and professional future. You might try to find local examples of family friends or professors who have studied or lived overseas to illustrate how study abroad has positively affected their lives. By formulating your arguments methodically, you will understand yourself and your reasons for studying abroad that much better.

The media often play up unfortunate incidents in student study and travel abroad. This is an ideal opportunity for you to research your destination in order to explain it to your parents and dispel the negative misconceptions with solid facts. You might also share information from professors and students who have gone to the same places or even from other parents. Give parents tips for researching the country themselves. Show them the health and safety guidelines set up by your institution's study abroad office, or by the Forum on Education Abroad and NAFSA, as discussed in Chapter 2. But their fears do have a basis. Before you leave, prepare a plan for communicating and handling any emergency—at home or abroad. Be sure to share with them all of your contact and other important information: your address and telephone number in the host country, medical information, your credit card numbers, your passport number, a photocopy of your passport, and contact information for the program's resident director, the program's U.S. office (many programs also have a twenty-four-hour telephone number), the study abroad office at your school, and the local U.S. embassy and consulate.

Parents have many other concerns about financing your experience, if you will graduate on time, or even how your day-to-day life will play out. Now is the time to hone your research skills and communicate clearly and responsibly with your family. Sometimes, though, you will be unable to obtain this information, and you will have to express to your parents that you cannot foresee everything, and that neither you nor they have control over every detail.

The study abroad experience can be used by you and your parents as a chance for greater maturity and learning on your part. You will become more independent. Embrace this opportunity, and let your parents know how you expect to grow. At the end of the day, this is *your* experience, and the best way for your family to help you succeed is by giving you room for independence.

Conclusion

Preparation for studying abroad is a multifaceted endeavor. It requires consideration of your academic core objectives, utilization of resources offered to you, and independent research. Prior academic work at your home institution, as well as predeparture orientations, will give you a means to begin your preparation in an organized manner. But a successful experience also involves what you do on your own—obtaining information from peers and networking, managing that information for yourself, and communicating it to others. These skills and experiences will not only help you prepare for studying abroad, but will help you to grow as a person as well.

Chapter Four
GETTING THE MOST
OUT OF YOUR EXPERIENCE

The big moment has arrived. You have selected a program, researched your destination, and taken care of all of the practical preparations for a term abroad. You fit everything into one or two suitcases, made your flight on time, and are ready to take those first steps in a new country and culture. Now what?

You know you want a significant study abroad experience, but how do you ensure this once you arrive? This chapter is about much more than just being there; it focuses on the achievement of academic goals and ways to reflect on your experience in the moment. Generally speaking, you can maximize the experience by remembering that it is part of a holistic educational journey linked to an academic foundation (see Figure 4.1). But how do you transition from simply living a parallel existence in another place—communicating with your friends at home daily on Skype and following the same routines you would at home—to true intercultural competence? Are you ready for personal transformations? Are you ready to learn about, understand, and respect your host culture? Are you ready to discover new and different ideas and gain new skills? Throughout this process, getting the most out of your experience means taking every opportunity for critical reflection about yourself and your place in the foreign culture.

Figure 4.1   The Global Classroom Learning Cycle

Understanding Culture

We have discussed "culture" in earlier chapters and the importance of both your home culture and those in which you will be studying. But what actually happens when you come face-to-face with the foreign culture? What are the steps to real cross-cultural understanding?

Your Cultural Identity in a Global Context

Your path to intercultural competence mirrors your travel abroad: it is a journey through various stages of cultural awareness and sensitivity toward a more developed worldview and sense of self. When you first arrive in the host country, it is natural to be focused internally, perhaps feeling isolated and relating cultural interactions to your personal background and individual interpretations. Even if you researched your new location, you still lack important *context*—the kind of understanding and respect for the issues and culture that begin to emerge for you in the first few months on the ground. Over time, as many other students have, you will become increasingly aware of your environment.[1] One begins to see similarities between the home culture and the foreign culture. Eventually, students begin to understand their personal cultures in the context of others, accepting differences without judging, adjusting behavior to fit better in the foreign culture, and hence gaining skills in communicating cross-culturally. This signifies being able to empathize with members of the host

culture, being increasingly able to "put oneself in the shoes" of others. As students are confronted with cultural difference, their global perspectives become progressively more complex and sophisticated.[2]

Some students will eventually feel integrated into the foreign culture, able to define themselves in multiple cultural contexts and to adapt to various cultural situations. They have gained what experts refer to as intercultural competence, or "a set of cognitive, affective and behavioral skills and characteristics that support effective and appropriate interaction in a variety of cultural contexts."[3] Not only will a widening global perspective be evident in interactions in the foreign culture, but it will also show up in personal development. An individual's development will be holistic—a combination of increased awareness and knowledge of the foreign culture, increased ease interacting with others, and more confidence in personal values and identity.

Dealing with Differences

This process of building intercultural competency on your holistic educational journey will have speed bumps. You will no doubt experience differences between your home and host cultures in relation to language, values, appearance, status, and numerous other factors. You may at first be surprised by the superficial differences you notice, and you may pass through stages of stress, irritation, fatigue, and shock. Experts call this "culture shock." It is a result of "the natural contradiction between our accustomed patterns of behavior and the psychological conflict of attempting to maintain them in the new cultural environment."[4]

According to Peter Adler, an expert in intercultural communication, "Culture shock is primarily a set of emotional reactions to the loss of perceptual reinforcements from one's own culture, to new cultural stimuli which have little or no meaning, and to the misunderstanding of new and diverse experiences."[5] These disturbances can be accompanied by feelings of homesickness, helplessness, isolation, and sadness, as well as hostility, irritability, sleeping and eating disturbances, and loss of focus. It is important to recognize these symptoms, be aware of the fact that they could be a result of this culture shock, and accept this phenomenon. Any significant change or loss, any transition, means that we are confronted with new processes and events that do not fit into our everyday, habitual frameworks. We might not have the tools to deal with these new occurrences, and might quickly feel overwhelmed.[6] But like all life-altering changes, the transition from one culture to another simultaneously is a source of anxiety and a path to personal growth.[7]

There are four generally recognized stages of culture shock:

1. *The honeymoon stage:* An initial stage of euphoria and excitement after arrival on-site where everything seems quaint, novel, new, and interesting.
2. *Culture stress and shock:* An individual moves through feelings of fatigue associated with practicing new behaviors in a new culture, as well as disorientation, irritability, rejection, isolation, helplessness, frustration, anxiety, or anger.
3. *Integration:* Possibly without even noticing, an individual recovers from the stressful situation and becomes more familiar with the subtleties of the new culture, feeling more comfortable functioning within it. Communication becomes easier; customs and behaviors become more understandable. Multiple worldviews may develop and coexist without any major anxiety or confusion.
4. *Adaptation and acceptance:* An individual develops an ability to function in the host culture with a decreased sense of foreignness, arriving at a comfortable stability and capacity to assimilate changes and accept things that cannot be changed.

Because transitions can recur, you might cycle through these stages a number of times throughout the study abroad experience.[8] For example, a new professor that you find challenging, a new section of a class, or even something as simple as a conversation with your host mother, can become a source of stress that might trigger the ups and downs of culture shock. Fortunately, culture shock is just a period of transition and change. It is more often than not temporary and you will be able to find the means to move on. The unfamiliar environment where you cannot fall back on any of your normal coping strategies will eventually become familiar to you. The introspection that is often triggered by a stressful situation helps you to become more self-aware and develop valuable critical thinking and communication skills.[9]

Overcoming Culture Shock

The first step to overcoming culture, or transition, shock is to realize that it may happen to you and to know that everyone experiences this shock

Alexandra Browning, SIT Study Abroad, China

differently or to varying degrees. What helps you cope and de-stress at home might help you in your new setting—talking with others, exercising, getting enough sleep, writing in a journal. Alternatively, you might have to find new, healthy coping mechanisms. Never hesitate to ask for help from on-site staff and friends, and be sure to develop a support network. Anxiety and a certain level of stress are inevitable, so try not to be too hard on yourself.

Furthermore, you can use this phenomenon as a learning experience. Consider writing entries in a blog or a journal where you note your successes in adapting and interacting—not just the difficult moments—and how these successes help you learn about your host culture and yourself. Be aware of your own cultural values, beliefs, behaviors, and assumptions. Then, take a step back to think about your new environment, how it is different and similar to what you know, which parts you like and dislike. Remain open-minded and withhold judgment, accept rather than reject, and be empathetic by trying to place yourself in the worldview of your host culture. By viewing this process and the culture you are confronted with as complex, you will be more likely to move from stress to adaptation and acceptance of cultural differences.[10] We offer ideas for reflection on this learning process in Worksheet 3: "Engaging with Your Experience" (featured in the Worksheets section) and later in this chapter.

Techniques discussed previously involving expectation management can be used while dealing with culture shock and the hurdles of adaptation. Constantly reevaluate your expectations as you obtain new information.[11] When you encounter an uncomfortable situation, think about your prior expectations. How did you expect the event to play out? Were your expectations reasonable? What can you do to reduce discomfort the next time a similar situation occurs? You might not always eat meals when you would like, stores are not necessarily open on Sundays or late at night, the Internet might be slow at times, or the traffic on the street outside your apartment might be very noisy. But when you adjust to and overcome these obstacles, you are one step further to being conscious of differences in the world around you.

Anticipating roadblocks in your cultural adjustment will help you deal with culture shock when it arrives. One of these hurdles, communication with home, might come as a surprise to you. In our age of the quick and accessible communication of Facebook, Skype, cell phones, and instant messaging, it is essential to discuss how communication with home affects your cultural adaptation. Maintaining links with home is essential, but it is a double-edged sword. Know that the time you spend talking with people at home means less time exploring the people and culture that actually surround you. This does not mean never talking to friends and family at home. Do keep them updated on your whereabouts and well-being, but set limits and expectations for yourself. Remember what communicating—or refraining from communicating—can do for you: breaking out of your comfort zone, communicating with locals, dealing with challenges on your own, and learning about the world beyond the "world wide web" will allow you to grow personally and intellectually.

You will continuously cycle through the stages of cultural learning and adjustment, from anticipating similarity to encountering shock, to opening yourself up to new possibilities, to internalizing and learning, to transcending boundaries and appreciating diversity.[12] By getting "culture shocked," you are challenging yourself, surpassing your comfort zone, and becoming much more aware of your identity and of the world around you. You are building skills, gaining confidence, and forging relationships that surpass your former boundaries. Ultimately, you are learning what it means to be a global citizen.

The Challenge of Communication in a Different Culture

Immersion in a new culture means more than just being present. It involves purposeful and thoughtful communication and interaction with the culture. The ups and downs of cross-cultural communication, when combined with the practical elements of adapting to a new environment, might be difficult for you to manage at times. Ineffective cultural communication can lead to greater culture shock and longer adaptation periods. For example, a negative cultural interaction might taint later interpretations or interactions with locals, instead of providing a learning experience about the culture. This, in turn, might provoke you to limit your interactions with locals, which would hinder further cultural learning.[13] Although it is not an easy task and may require practice, being aware of your interactions with the host culture and your emotional and behavioral responses to these encounters is the first step to turning the potentially negative moments into learning experiences.

Regardless of the native language of your country of study, you are bound to run into challenges when communicating with your hosts. These challenges originate from a number of common assumptions and human tendencies.[14] For example, most of us want to think that others are similar to us, that all people are the same. With the increasing Westernization of the world, this tendency is more and more widespread. But it is not because someone dresses like you or listens to the same music as you that nonverbal behavior, values, and beliefs will be the same. Instead of assuming similarities, which might lead to deception at some point, anticipate differences with others. Similarly, although you might recognize a certain behavior, this does not mean that it has the same meaning for your host as it has for you. A nod or the "OK" hand signal might not represent the same thing for you as it does for the person in front of you. What you express may not be what your host understands, and what you understand may not be what the other person is trying to express. Another of our tendencies is to evaluate instead of simply understanding the worldview of others. While understanding—or trying to understand—a foreign behavior is essential, you do not have to accept or agree with it. But you can seek to understand its origins.

Michael Rankin, IES Abroad, Granada, Spain

It is easy to dwell on the uncomfortable misunderstanding, but rec-ognizing cultural communication success is also important not only to learning, but to your self-esteem and well-being abroad. Effective cross-cultural communication, although assuredly presenting numerous chal-lenges, is an important skill that will help you practically in the future, and it will also allow you to learn about your host culture and about yourself.

Personal and Cultural Identity

Studying abroad is most definitely about discovering another culture, another language, another place. But it is also about exploring who you are, about becoming more aware of your individuality and your identity. Recall Slimbach's description of the transcultural journey from Chapter 1. The path toward developing a transcultural identity begins with an inward quest to discover oneself: "Being a transcultural learner is not first about our outward-moving actions to study language, collect cultural information, or deliver development services. It is foremost about how we go about these activities, and the character of our own personal life in the process."[15] Just as your personal identity affects how and what you take from your experience abroad, the interaction of foreign culture learning, learning about oneself, and skills development results in a transformed personal identity.

The challenge for many U.S. students is to overcome their own cultural conditioning and norms in intercultural situations. Cultural norms, based on values that seem inherent and instinctive, are strong. The mature, prepared student must be able to look beyond personal norms and to let reflection about a situation overcome instinctive tendencies.[16] Putting your own "truths" aside and putting yourself in the place of the other person will help you to develop true empathy. Such behaviors and qualities are not simple to adopt, but they may come more easily thanks to extended contact with other cultures. Some local cultural norms you may admire and implement for yourself; others you may merely adapt to; and others you may never be able to accept, as they are too different from and contrary to your personal beliefs and values. As you develop and mature, you will be able to recognize these types of interactions and behaviors and become more aware of your own viewpoints and principles.[17] According to experts Rebecca Hovey and Adam Weinberg: "As students engage with communities abroad, notions of global citizenship provide powerful transformative opportunities to explore one's own identity, lifelong commitments and allegiances. . . . As students from the United States leave the immediate communities of their home towns and college campuses, they build new allegiances that form part of their identity as global citizens."[18]

Ultimately, exploration of your own identity plays a role in developing a sense of global citizenship.

Being "American" Abroad: Learning About Your Cultural Identity

Even with optimistic expectations, and the most well-founded tools for integrating into a new culture, being an American abroad is challenging. This is especially true in countries where inequality with the United States is flagrant and you are confronted constantly with the "privilege" of being American. Just as you want to discuss their country, your hosts will want to talk about what it feels like to be an American, about government and politics, current events, the economy, religion, history, the media, foreign policy, or education. Just as you have surely formed opinions about the country where you are studying based on what you have seen in the media, your hosts will also have an opinion of the United States founded on information from the Internet, television, or a past visit to the country. Do not be surprised if your host family asks you about the size of houses in your neighborhood back home or how many guns your family owns.

Just as you might have stereotypes about your host culture, you are bound to be confronted with stereotypes about Americans, not all of which are positive. We have all heard the term "ugly American." What does this mean? Originally, *The Ugly American* was the title of a novel written in 1958 by Eugene Burdick and William Lederer about U.S. failure to battle communism in Southeast Asia due to a lack of understanding of the local culture there. It has come to describe an American abroad who is materialistic, condescending, and self-righteous, expecting that others conform to the values in our consumer-driven society. You might be seen as hardworking and motivated, but you might also face stereotypes of being loud, immature, wealthy, obsessed with work, and ignorant of other countries.

Studies show that students react in various manners to the challenge of the American identity.[19] First, thanks to predeparture orientations on how *not* to be the ugly American, many students counter this ethnocentric attitude by trying to blend in as much as possible and avoiding "typically American" behaviors. When interrogated about American politics (the war in Iraq, for example) students tend to distance themselves from government policy. Such conversation provides students with a venue for acting as a "good" American: open and accepting of others' opinions. Many students enter into the study abroad experience with just a mere notion of American identity and nationality. But time spent abroad can deepen this understanding. So, in addition to language learning and cultural understanding, your development of American national identity is equally important in your study abroad experience. This can then serve as a stepping-stone to greater global awareness.

How can you avoid being stereotyped as the "ugly American"? You can start by being familiar with yourself, the cultural baggage you bring with you, and your cultural identity, politics, and society. For example, read international newspapers and listen to foreign newscasts online to become knowledgeable about U.S. and world events. Learn the language of your hosts as a demonstration of respect. But of course, don't be afraid to be yourself and keep your own values and viewpoints so long as you are respectful, tolerant, and curious about others. If an interaction feels threatening or uncomfortable, trust your instincts and steer clear; but if the conversation about even controversial topics seems good-natured, use it as an opportunity to learn and teach.

How you interact and exchange ideas with people you meet—from other local or international students to your host family—not only will affect their opinion of the United States, but will also teach you about interacting with others in general. You will learn about yourself as an individual—your beliefs and values, and how you are American. You will be forced to evaluate and reevaluate your beliefs based on conversations with others. You will learn how the United States and also how *you* personally fit into a larger picture.

Being Yourself Abroad: Personal Identity

You know that identity is multidimensional. Gender, ability, race, sexual orientation, ethnicity, and religious beliefs are only some of the many facets of identity. The way that individuals from other countries view these components of your identity can also help you learn about the host culture and about yourself.

In order to ensure your comfort and safety and best integrate into the culture, research the culture before you arrive and then observe your hosts' behavior and appearance. For example, the majority of study abroad participants are women, but attitudes toward women vary immensely in different cultures. This might include strong gender roles in the workforce, in the family, at school, or in public. Making eye contact, smiling, or wearing certain clothes can have profound meaning in your country of study. Likewise, sexual orientation is something viewed very differently in different cultures. You should research customs for any social situation—from dating to friendship—in your country of study. Look into gay, lesbian, bisexual, transsexual, and cross-gender resources for your destination. Know if and how you should go about disclosing your preferences and the effects this may have on your relationship with others.

Although many elements of cultural adaptation will be similar to fellow students, racially diverse students might experience culture shock in a different manner. Every culture defines race and ethnicity differently and has a different attitude toward race issues. Just as discrimination may be a valid concern in your country of study, curiosity might also be an important challenge. You might be the first person of a different ethnicity that a local has ever seen. Often, this can serve as a liberating learning experience: students abroad report that other elements of identity such as sex, religious affiliation, and class can take precedence over ethnicity. Students are seen more as a "foreigner" or "American" than as African American, Hispanic, or Asian. Or, depending on the location, you might blend in more or in an entirely different manner than you do in the United States.[20]

For every student, studying abroad means adapting to the customs and laws of your host country, even if they are profoundly different from what you are used to. This might translate into discovering a new freedom to express your identity, or confronting difficult restrictions and ideas. It involves observing those around you, staying safe and healthy, and balancing your values with those of your hosts. How you express yourself and react to difficult situations can become an undeniably meaningful opportunity for learning and personal growth.

Success in the Global Classroom

Once you are on-site, you can easily recall the four dimensions of the global classroom to find practical methods of adapting to your host country, learning about your cultural and personal identity, and generally ensuring your success.

Dimensions of the Learning Cycle

Personal and Cultural Identity
Know yourself, and be in tune with yourself. Be sure to find your particular balance of academics and extracurricular activities, for example.

But if you feel you might be having problems coping, be sure to consult on-site staff. Also, interaction with fellow study abroad students can be an effective outlet for culture shock and a means for comparing cultural observations and interpretations. But beware of resorting to the group in order to avoid interactions with locals or the challenges of cultural understanding and learning.

Experiential and Vocational Development

Remember that the skills you have learned throughout your college career up until now can help you abroad. For example, manage your time effectively to avoid unnecessary stress. Use problem-solving skills to find your way around the subway system. Use communication skills you learned with your college roommate as you interact with your new roommates or host family. Academically, you might have to adapt your study skills to the new university environment. For example, in Spain you might be expected to memorize and regurgitate information, but in England there is more in-class discussion. Be sure to ask professors or the on-site staff for help if you need it.

Global Citizenship

Take every opportunity for cultural interaction during your time abroad in order to get the most out of your experience. You can learn about the foreign culture through your homestay, through excursions and cultural activities, or through internships or volunteering. Take advantage of unstructured opportunities for learning also: see a play, go to the movies with friends, join a club, play a sport, or strike up a conversation with the student sitting next to you in the lecture hall. Always observe others, ask questions, and be curious and open-minded in your interactions. Engaging in your day-to-day activities with the people and culture around you is the first step to engaging on a larger scale as a global citizen.

The Importance of Active Reflection

As discussed in Chapter 1, John Dewey introduced the idea of experiential education, stating that heightened learning can result from hands-on experience. The experiential learning cycle espoused by Dewey (and later, many other scholars) usually begins with a concrete experience.[21] You are likely in the midst of that right now. But experience is not only what happens in your current reality—it is also the interaction of the present with your past and future. You interpret the present with the lens

J. P. Kaderbek, SIT Study Abroad, Morocco

of the past and carry the present on into future interactions. Active reflection involves thinking about the four dimensions of your learning experience: your personal identity, your cultural identity, vocational and skills learning, and global citizenship.

Journaling is one useful and practical method of purposeful reflection leading to personal growth and development. It helps create a private space for your thoughts.[22] It is a means to vent, to reflect, to maintain a certain awareness, to give order to events and feelings, and to put thoughts and emotions in perspective. It is a way to make connections, to become the historian for your own life, but also to move from introspection to connecting with the outside world through observation and reflection.

In a study conducted of Chinese students participating in a short-term program in Oxford, England, participants were instructed to keep a diary recording observations and reflections on daily activities, elements related to their coursework, stressful or challenging experiences, and strategies used to overcome difficulties or cope with stress.[23] Across the board, students reported incidents of culture shock, difficulty interacting with locals and adjusting to a different lifestyle, and cultural or communication misunderstandings. Students also revealed in their journals their methods for overcoming and coping with these challenges, along with strategies for communication and meeting new people, proof of awareness of cultural differences, acceptance of differences, development of social skills and self-confidence, increased engagement with the new and different environment, and displays of openness and curiosity. In this case, the introspection of journaling appeared to facilitate cultural comparisons and then understanding and recognition of personal growth and achievements.

Less research has been done on blogging, but it has clearly become a more popular medium for today's student. Given the interactive nature of blogging, we can extrapolate to say that it offers a social support system as well as an opportunity for internal reflection. Blogs provide a forum for sharing emotions and thoughts, and discussing distressing events in a way unlike face-to-face communication. Blogs can help you create a network with other students, allow you to keep friends and family at home updated on your experiences and well-being, or even act as a call for help if you are in distress.[24] However, every moment spent on the computer, at your desk, and in your room is a moment not spent interacting with your new friends or your host family, exploring your environment, and taking full advantage of your time abroad. It is essential to use interactive communication technology wisely, as a place for directed reflection on your experience.

Active reflection can take on many forms, from writings in a paper-and-pencil notebook or on the back of your train ticket to an online blog hosted by your school or a study abroad website. E-mails written to your family in the United States also fit the bill. Your reflections might include a list of what you did on a certain day, or a description of children playing in a park, or how you felt in the shadow of the Coliseum in Rome. What is important is that you engage actively in your role as a "cultural ethnographer"—observing, making inferences, turning them into hypotheses, testing those hypotheses, and transforming those into generalizations to help you in your understanding of and adaptation to a foreign culture.

Scholars have developed ethnographic research methods, such as O.D.I.S. (Observe, Describe, Interpret, Suspend Judgment) and D.I.E. (Description, Interpretation, Evaluation), that can help you work purposefully at becoming more culturally aware while gaining observation skills. As you reflect actively, first observe verbal and nonverbal cues. Then, mentally describe to yourself what is happening, or what you see, or how you feel. Next, create various interpretations based on your personal worldview to help yourself make sense of the observation and descriptions. Finally, put yourself in your hosts' shoes to attempt to understand them and yourself: you might acknowledge your discomfort with the unfamiliar situation, decide to observe similar events, consult others for feedback, or respect differences and defer judgment. Whether you use this process in your journal or just as a quick run-through in your mind as you observe an unfamiliar occurrence, it will help you to adapt better to any situation and appreciate your personal interpretation of it. It allows you to take a quick step back from an event, and hopefully reduce the discomfort associated with culture shock. By thinking about your experience through different lenses, you can get a more holistic picture of what is going on around you. Put simply, active reflection in any form will help you develop in all four dimensions of your academic growth.

These are just some examples among many that will allow you to develop academically and personally during your experience abroad. Recall our discussion about your goals for study abroad. Use all of what your program offers and what you discover in your host country to meet these goals—be it everyday cultural discoveries, courses, pedagogical styles, living arrangements, field trips, or friendships. Apply old tools and seek out new ones for adapting and learning—and sometimes coping. It is up to you to adopt and develop your own techniques based on advice here, from your program, from your home institution, and from your peers.

Ensuring Your Health and Safety Abroad

No matter how much you prepare psychologically and academically, no matter how solid your intentions are to have a meaningful and transformative experience, ensuring your health and safety is essential to a positive and successful term abroad. Due to the emotional stress of culture shock, coupled with the physical stress of living in a new environment, students are prone to minor and major ailments and risky situations. Without staying in your room or failing to partake in one-of-a-kind learning experiences, take responsibility for your own actions and decisions by following basic precautions and using common sense.

Studying abroad is the ideal time to explore historic districts of your city or meet new friends at the local pub. Be sure to do so with common sense and caution to guarantee a successful experience. Common sense means being constantly aware of your surroundings and avoiding unnecessary risks. And your surroundings include all of what is going on around you: what people are saying, which neighborhoods are dangerous, where you can get help, and what is culturally acceptable or not. When you use common sense you are not throwing caution to the wind

Sage Weaver, Volunteer Organization's Special Needs, Santa Cruz, Bolivia

as a result of being overcome by the excitement of being in a new environment. Hitchhiking and unsafe sex are no safer in a foreign country than they are at home. Never assume anything simply because someone you meet on a bus or at a bar speaks English well or seems very friendly. Those characteristics may not be a good enough reason to walk home with her or him that evening. Behave in a manner that is respectful to those around you and to yourself. Heed the advice and warnings of your local friends, your host family, and your program—they often know better than you the risks of attending a political protest going on in the center of town, of frequenting a certain neighborhood, or of wearing a certain type of clothing. Always keep someone, such as your friends, parents, and your program, aware of your whereabouts and contact information. Finally, remember that crime can happen anywhere, but as a foreigner you become much more of a target.

As noted earlier, you are an ambassador of your country, your school, and your program. As such, you should be aware of appropriate standards of conduct. You have taken on a personal obligation to follow certain program guidelines and local laws. Misconduct, such as jeopardizing your well-being or that of other students; abusing local laws and customs; or using, purchasing, or selling illegal substances, can result in very serious repercussions, from dismissal from the program to arrest.

Consumption of alcohol is of particular concern, as excessive use impairs your judgment, making you a target for other risks to your health and safety. Whether it is due to the lower drinking age, an uninformed idea of alcohol use in the host country, peer pressure, or a coping strategy for stress or depression, unhealthy use of alcohol occurs abroad, just as it does on college campuses in the United States. Each year several hundred Americans are arrested while abroad on drug charges, or even die due to drug or alcohol abuse or related incidents.[25] The following statistics show the severity of U.S. college drinking and drug abuse, which extend to study abroad as well:

- 300,000 current college students will die of alcohol-related causes like drunk driving or health problems.
- On average, a student spends about $900 per year on alcohol (compared to an average of $450 on books).
- One-third of students report having missed at least one class due to alcohol or drug use, and one-quarter have failed a test or project because of it.

- 90 percent of campus rapes happen when either the victim or the aggressor has used alcohol.
- 70 percent of college students report having engaged in sexual activity that they would not have if they had not been using alcohol.[26]

Besides health issues surrounding alcohol and other drug usage, this phenomenon is also cultural, and as with other cultural issues, you will grapple with it while abroad. In France, it is normal and sociable for people of all ages to drink a glass or two of wine with dinner, but somewhat rare to see extremely intoxicated university-age students on the streets. In some North African countries, it is looked down upon for women to drink alcohol at all. Not to mention that legal blood alcohol levels and laws surrounding drug and alcohol use are often different in foreign countries. Ignorance of the laws in your host country will not hold up as an excuse in the local courts. As with all cultural norms, you should observe what is going on around you in order to best understand and integrate into the host culture, always keeping in mind your health and safety.

From the perspective of your physical health, be aware of your body and how you are feeling, using your best judgment and never hesitating to get help. The experience of being overseas is bound to be taxing for you, from the moment you step off the plane and suffer from jet lag to the time when a new food just does not sit right on your stomach or the stress of speaking a foreign language exhausts you. Expect to feel sick and tired from time to time, make space for culture shock and the ups and downs of transition, and communicate with program administrators and friends. Following a good health plan is essential: eat right and exercise regularly, avoid alcohol and substance abuse, be aware of emotional issues and your psychological responses, get enough sleep, and seek medical help when you need it. You should have researched the health risks of your location of study: remain aware of these in your daily choices, from where you fill up your water bottle to taking your malaria medication as directed.

Special consideration should be given to mental health abroad. Often, the new stressors of study abroad, such as loss and separation, unforeseen situations, lack of familiar coping mechanisms, changes in medication, and new and different social pressures, can result in mental health concerns. When symptoms and risk factors interfere with daily life and normal functioning, all students, whether they have suffered from mental illness in the past or not, should seek out help from on-site program staff and consider consulting a mental health professional. All students can benefit from some tips to maintain good mental health: stay active, maintain good nutrition and sleeping habits, balance work and leisure, and stay connected to family and friends on-site and at home. Be sure to bring along sufficient medication for the duration of your stay and documentation from your doctor about your illness. Sharing your concerns with staff or close friends who can help you or notice dangerous symptoms can be a useful coping mechanism as well.[27]

Conclusion

No matter how well prepared, you will hit glitches in your experience abroad. You will make mistakes with the language, you may not greet a new friend in an appropriate manner, or you may be upset by how someone treats you. This is normal! Indeed, these kinds of experiences happen in your everyday life back home. So, do not be too hard on yourself. Take a step back, then walk around the event and start anew. Try to make as many connections as possible—between your feelings, your personal life, your academics, your home culture, and your host culture. This will allow you to understand and grow from your experiences. Sure, some of your best memories may *not* involve listening to a lecture. But students who make connections between all aspects of their academic and nonacademic lives report a more fulfilling and satisfying experience abroad.[28]

Even with all the practical tips and academic theory under your belt, there are some simple elements that will ensure your success abroad: your curiosity about the culture, your generosity and desire to learn, how you manage your expectations, your acceptance of the unexpected and the gray areas, your willingness to understand another's viewpoint, and your knowledge about your cultural identity and yourself.

Chapter Five
REORIENTATION

Welcome home! You have completed a rewarding study abroad program. It may seem like the world has opened up to you and there are unlimited new opportunities. But here is the catch: simply going abroad does not guarantee the realization of intercultural competency and personal development. Indeed, research shows that by talking about and reflecting on your experiences *after* returning home, you can gain a much deeper perspective of your experience, of yourself, and of the world. Many students who return from abroad believe the experience helped them; they gained maturity, independence, and some problem-solving skills. Yet many also say it is difficult to contextualize exactly how the experience will fit into their long-term education, career, or life goals.

This chapter acknowledges that reorientation is a very important part of your educational journey. Once again, we emphasize a link between this phase and your holistic academic plan (see Figure 5.1). The chapter describes how the reentry can be shocking and disorienting, and it explores the dynamics of reverse-entry experiences. It also discusses institutional support as well as personal steps that you can take to address reentry challenges. Ultimately, this chapter is about ways to see study abroad as a beginning, not as an end in itself.

Stages of Reorientation

Studies show that there are identifiable stages to the reorientation process for many students, including:

Figure 5.1 The Global Classroom Learning Cycle

- *Disengagement*, or the process you go through when you begin thinking about returning home and leaving friends on the program.
- *Reentry*, or the "honeymoon phase," when you typically feel excitement and euphoria about returning home.
- *Reverse culture shock*, often a period of dampened euphoria. The shock of the return to your home culture can produce all kinds of emotions, sometimes even a sense of alienation or frustration.
- *Readjustment and assessment* occur as you begin to process your feelings and gradually settle back into life in your home culture. As we will discuss later in this chapter, the readjustment phase is the one most associated with critical reflection on the experience, identity, and responsibilities of a global citizen.[1]

Disengagement

The process of transitioning out of your study abroad experience begins *before* you have even left the host country. If you have lived abroad for months, even years, the return can seem profound. It is easy to be affected emotionally by the wide-reaching arc of your study abroad experience.

The conclusion of your time abroad will lead to a period of disengagement that may include final meetings with new friends, visits to your favorite sites or hangouts one last time, and packing for home. This is actually the start of an opportunity for reflecting on how much you may have grown from the experience, often in ways both expected and unexpected.

As part of the journey home many students plan their actual return for well after the formal end of their study program. Students often take the opportunity to extend their stay by traveling further afield from their host country or by visiting with new friends from foreign countries. Regardless of the reasons for extension, though, students who conduct some sort of final tour are, in effect, beginning the end of their journey.

The homeward journey itself is typically one full of mixed emotions—from sadness at leaving what had become so comfortable abroad to relief upon returning to familiar surroundings of home. In taking that first step toward home, some students will promise to return often to their host country (and some will even do so); some will hope to return with family members one day; a few will vow never to return again. By any measure, the process of preparing to return home and "cleaning up one's affairs" in a foreign country can be the beginning of a surprisingly emotional transition.

Reentry, or the "Honeymoon Phase"

The second stage of reorientation involves sharing your experiences with others and starting to translate them to your life at home. It also represents an opportunity to link the experience back to your academic development. If you are like many other returnees, you will feel a personal sense of excitement in returning home and reconnecting with your friends and loved ones. And you will report that you had a "satisfying" experience. This means different things to different people, of course, but some common indicators of satisfaction include achievement of educational goals, personal development, friendships, traveling, and gaining valuable skills.

Just think back for a moment on what you have achieved. Months or even years ago, you selected a program to enroll in outside your native experience. You went through a detailed application process that included framing the experience within your broader program of study. You began to transition to the mindset you would need to survive in that new environment and embarked on your journey. You performed well in classes in a foreign country, some of which were taught in a way that was quite different from what you were used to. You also traveled to places and developed friendships you might not have experienced otherwise. In other words, you set an important goal and found a way to achieve it. This sense of pride is an important part of the reentry phase.

Reentry is also about enjoying being home and sharing your recent experiences with others. And *please do share your experiences*: it is essential for a healthy reorientation process that you are able to communicate about your experience. One of the more important networks for sharing and processing experiences can be with like-minded peer groups—other returnees at your college or university from study abroad programs around the world. Some students actually find that they have more in common now with students they didn't know before who are also grappling with the same issues of transition. Beyond family and friends, be sure to also talk with professors and study abroad professionals on campus about your experience. This will help you to connect with other people and other opportunities of which you might not be aware. The process of sharing will also help you develop communication skills and begin to interpret complex feelings and understandings of the experience.

Remember that while reconnecting with friends and family can be joyful, it can also be difficult at times. Regardless of the length of time you have been away (a year, a semester, one quarter, or even one month), *you will see things differently than before*. And with that new perspective, you will find that some things have changed. For example, it is very likely that your friends have begun to adjust to life without you and that you will need to reacquaint yourself with their lifestyles and patterns. In some rare circumstances, college students learn upon their return that their friends have "moved on," either to a new routine and peer group or perhaps to a boyfriend or girlfriend, leaving the returnee feeling slightly left out.

Finally, one part of reentry often creates special frustrations: you may notice that there is a limit to the attention others will devote to your stories. No matter how exciting, exotic, or profound the experiences you have had, others will be less engaged in listening to or reflecting on them with you. This may be a function of many factors, ranging from the benign, such as limited time and preoccupations on the part of your listeners, to the more serious—ethnocentrism on the part of some U.S. citizens, limited knowledge or understanding, or even jealousy at the experience you have had. Even if you are lucky to have the perfect friend who is interested in much of what you have experienced, her reception of your stories will lack important context. Put simply, it may seem impossible for anyone else to understand the depth and quality of the experience you have had. These are but a few of the frustrations that can contribute to a third stage of reorientation: reverse culture shock.

Reverse Culture Shock

The transitions involved in study abroad—in preparing for departure, settling in to the new culture of your host country, and returning home—can be dramatic. Kevin Gaw defines reverse culture shock as "the process of readjusting, reacculturating, and reassimilating into one's own home culture after living in a different culture for a significant period of time."[2] This also represents a prime opportunity for learning and reflecting on the experience in relation to your academic goals.

Through studying and living abroad for a prolonged period of time, you have changed. You are one of a small number of American citizens who have had this transformative experience; you have connected with another culture and way of life. You know and understand much more about the world than some of your peers. And you may naturally find yourself thinking back on your experience living in a foreign culture. You may wonder what your friends are up to in your host country, how

Lauren Merriman, Wooster in Chiang Mai, Thailand

your host family is doing today, and so on. These feelings of being transported in your mind to another place are one of the things that make study abroad such a special experience. All of this can be unsettling, but it is perfectly natural. We encourage returnees to *own* their feelings and, whenever they have the opportunity, to communicate with others about concerns regarding this change.

You are not alone in experiencing reverse culture shock. Some of the earliest research on this phenomenon in the United States actually dates back to the World War II period, when psychologists found military veterans facing challenges in their transition back to normal life at home. This research influenced theories of psychology and anthropology and eventually worked its way into higher education studies examining student returnees in studies in the decades that followed.[3] One of the most fascinating, useful studies of the education abroad reentry experience was conducted by Bruce Labrack. Drawing on hundreds of data points, he identified a set of major reentry challenges for college students returning home from study abroad.[4] As you review this list, think about which of these resonates with you most, and why.

1. *Boredom:* After the excitement and newness of your time abroad, coming back to your old friends and routine can seem dull. Life was very exciting when you were studying abroad, so now a day trip to Portland seems pretty ordinary.
2. *"No one wants to hear":* It may seem like people at home do not want to listen to your stories; they may lose interest quickly after hearing the highlights of your experience.
3. *You can't explain:* Given the richness of your experience, you may find it difficult and frustrating to try to express the depth of your feelings to others.
4. *Reverse homesickness:* You will find yourself missing the people, places, and things that you enjoyed on-site, just as you missed home when you were away.
5. *Relationships have changed:* A natural shift in relationships may occur because you have changed during your time abroad, and most likely your friends and family at home have changed as well.
6. *People see the "wrong" changes:* Some may interpret the small changes in your behavior and ideas as a "bad" result of your time away.

7. *People misunderstand:* Others may misinterpret your words or behavior—helping in the kitchen, the way you dress, using a foreign language—as aggression or even showing off.

8. *Feelings of alienation:* Your image of home does not live up to your expectations, your home culture has faults that you did not notice before, or you are more critical of people and things.

9. *Inability to apply new knowledge and skills:* You may not find the opportunities you crave to use the newfound linguistic, social, or practical skills you learned during your experience.

10. *Loss or compartmentalization of the experience:* Between the stress of school, family, and friends, you may be frightened that your experiences will be lost or compartmentalized, like photos or a scrapbook.[5]

These issues range from the mundane to the very significant. Some of the challenges noted here can contribute to reverse culture shock during reentry.

Two other dimensions of reverse culture shock are noteworthy as well: (1) it can set in rather quickly; and (2) ironically, it can deeply affect those who got the most out of their study abroad experience. At its extreme, the emotions of exhilaration at being home may be quickly replaced by stress, value confusion, alienation, hostility, helplessness, and even depression.[6] There is often a shorter "honeymoon phase" for returnees than the period of exhilaration they experienced when first arriving overseas. And ironically, experts tell us, "those who adjusted best and were the most successful overseas usually experience the greatest amount of difficulty with reverse culture shock." In the face of such frustration, some returnees may "engage in 'flight' behavior. . . . They may withdraw from others, fantasize about returning overseas, or sleep a good deal."[7]

In summary, many students experience some challenges upon reentry. The first step in addressing them is recognizing that they are common and natural extensions of study abroad. Experts tell us that dealing with the stress of any transition can be much more manageable if it is anticipated in advance. Ultimately, we encourage you to try to recognize and come to accept these issues as they arise in your life. In Chapter 6 we outline how working through the reentry process constructively can also help refine your plans for personal and professional growth.

Readjustment and Reflection

Some people feel nearly as lost returning home as they did when arriving in their host country. Experts tell us there are both identifiable causes and symptoms of this phenomenon. And if one sees the transitions involved in study abroad as part of a process of self-discovery and education, it seems easy to conclude that the benefits dramatically outweigh the costs. As Weaver argues, "Reactions to the stress of cross-cultural adjustment are simply necessary 'growing pains' that eventually lead to greater emotional and intellectual maturity, a more flexible personality, and a wider global perspective."[8]

The fourth stage of reentry, readjustment and reflection, is critical, and it provides an opportunity to meaningfully contextualize your experience in relation to your academic goals. Typically, it is only after you have experienced some of the other stages that you can really begin to reflect on what the study abroad experience has meant to you. This stage of reflection is important for the purposes of processing your immediate experience, and it will help you to develop life and professional skills.

Meaningful Reflection and Assessment

Returning home can be a powerful experience. As noted in previous chapters, we recommend reflection on at least four key dimensions of learning through the study abroad experience: personal identity, cultural identity, experiential and vocational learning, and global citizenship. Individuals can evaluate their learning outcomes across these four dimensions in their own personal reflections, or they may be employed as part of a more formal, institutional reentry program.

Personal Identity

The first step in meaningful reflection on study abroad is to consider how you have changed. Your personal identity has been shaped by a combination of your experiences over the years—the most recent of which was study abroad. In Chapter 1 we invited you to reflect on your personal identity in light of the potential for the study abroad experience to transform your worldview. Readjustment provides an opportunity for critical

Figure 5.2 Dimensions of the Global Classroom

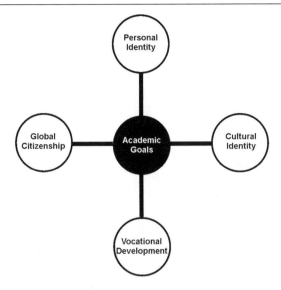

reflection on just that: who you are and how you may have changed through the experience. For example, looking back, why did you want to study abroad and how much did the experience fulfill your expectations? And what have you learned about your own worldview through the process of study abroad and travel? Recall some of the questions posed:

- Why are you curious about other regions or countries of the world?
- Do you consider yourself to be open-minded?
- Do you identify yourself as someone who can make a difference in the world?
- Are you generally optimistic or pessimistic?
- Are you multilingual?
- Are you environmentally conscious?
- Are you flexible? Do you adapt easily to new circumstances?
- Do you relate well to others?
- How do you picture yourself using this experience when you return?

Now that you have studied abroad and had an opportunity to reflect on your experiences, how would you answer these questions differently? And how do your answers relate to long-term plans for your education or career development? Worksheet 4 ("When You Return") provides a structured format to address questions in relation to all four dimensions of the experience.

Study abroad has also impacted your sense of identity and your role in peer groups, on campus, and in the community. You have probably returned to campus with even greater motivation to share with others. You may, for example, become more active as a tutor to other students, interact more with professors outside of class, create new social ties, become more politically active, or change in various other ways. In addition, you are probably more sensitive to diversity now that you have actually lived for a period as a "foreign" student and perhaps a minority. Since 2006, the Study Abroad for Global Engagement (SAGE) research project has set out to look at the long-term effects of study abroad for college students. Researchers have found that students do, in fact, become more "globally engaged" citizens, defined in terms of "the contributions a person makes to the common good by means of civic engagement, knowledge production, social entrepreneurship, and philanthropy." Students who have studied abroad report higher rates of active engagement in their communities with the hopes of making a difference and bettering the world around them.[9]

Cultural Identity

If a person's identity is shaped to some degree by social and cultural ties, then traveling outside your native experience gave you a unique opportunity to reflect on where you came from, in addition to your host culture. Study abroad can help you think about your own identity relative to local, national, and even global affiliations. There are many different aspects of culture. In terms of political and social views, for example, how has the experience influenced your view on issues like health care, immigration policy, school funding, and the U.S. war on terror? Given what you have observed in foreign cultures, how does the United States fare in taking care of its citizens? Are divisions between identity groups in foreign cultures worse or better than those in the United States, and why? And as an informal ambassador of the United States, were you able to articulate your ideas on themes like the current political, social, and cultural climate in the United States? How did you explain your views on these matters when asked by foreign students or perhaps your host family?

Study abroad also gives you a unique perspective on foreign cultures. When reflecting on cross-cultural learning it is often fascinating to begin with similarities and differences between cultures. Here are a few examples of topics for comparison:

- What are the main similarities between your host country and your home country? What are the main differences?
- How would you describe your host country's government and the level of citizen activism and engagement?
- What are the similarities and differences in terms of social and community ties?
- How do different cultures approach traditions and rituals differently?
- How do family and friends relate to one another differently across cultures?
- Is there a common sense of empowerment of the individual?
- Is there a significant difference in the consumer culture or materialism?

Reflection on these questions may help you to further articulate your ideas about foreign cultures and experiences. You may delve even deeper into issues of values and beliefs of the foreign culture. Did you find, for example, that there is truly a great deal of individualism in the host culture? Was the culture open and reflective? The ability to see individuals as different from common stereotypes and generalizations is, in fact, a skill in cross-cultural literacy.[10] This is also a great way to learn about and experience culture in all its fascinating dimensions.

Vocational Development

This third dimension relates to one of your primary reasons for studying abroad in the first place: to learn more about a specific topic or discipline, or to develop a skill such as language proficiency. While we recognize the centrality of the educational objectives of your experience in the abstract, it sometimes becomes secondary in terms of reflection and read-justment. By this we mean that it is less directly linked to your personal, social, and psychological development.

We have argued that there is no better way to gain specific knowl-edge, skills, and training than through direct, experiential learning. Study abroad can help students learn firsthand about topics in disciplines rang-ing from comparative literature, culture, politics, society, and the arts to science, language, and religion. And many disciplines have highly specific skill sets that can be attained through study abroad. Foreign language immersion and training are certainly foremost among these. Have you noticed that these skills have developed for you? Are you more able to take advantage of related interdisciplinary training, such as linking inter-national economics and business classes with Japanese language? If you participated in a specialized program, such as a course specifically focused on music composition, engineering, computer science, museum cura-tion, or poetry writing, how will you bring these newfound skills back to your home campus? Think about the specific skills you have gained during your experience, and how they can benefit you at home.

Global Citizenship

Your cross-cultural learning experience has promoted greater under-standing of yourself and others. You likely have a larger social circle, including citizens of foreign countries, based on your education abroad. You may even have an altered sense of "community" or "family," for example, as an extension of immersion in a foreign culture. You may have begun to change your behavior in areas you had not imagined before traveling abroad—perhaps becoming more environmentally conscious or more of a risk-taker. Regardless of the specific nature of the changes you have experienced, it is very likely that overseas study has inspired you to think more broadly about responsibilities as a global citizen.

We all begin our lives with a local perspective, and Chapter 1 dis-cussed ways that socialization can produce ethnocentrism. Much of this is good, understandable, even natural. But it is often quite narrow. As anthropologists Philip DeVita and James Armstrong stress, "The cultural assumptions we grow up with are powerful . . . speaking the same lan-guage, following the accepted patterns of behavior, embedded in a way of life, we tend to take many aspects of our own social action for granted.

. . . We are wonderfully successful performers on this complex and often confounding stage of sociocultural life."[11] Thus, our beliefs, associations, and routines help shape our basic cultural identity.

However, study abroad provides a special (and surprisingly rare) opportunity to learn more about the world. By crossing cultures and expanding your boundaries you have entered into a powerful educational environment from which you are unlikely to emerge without change. That is, the experience of living abroad—where values and traditions and standards are different from those that you grew up with—fosters cognitive dissonance. You were forced to grapple with your own identity and

Jessica Marsh, Syracuse University Abroad, Florence, Italy

those of others. And getting the most out of your experience means taking every opportunity for critical reflection about yourself and your place in the world, even after your return home.

Thus, study abroad can help promote a warmer embrace of collective, global citizenship. Larry Samovar and Richard Porter argue that it is essential that "we develop communication skills and abilities that are appropriate to a multicultural society and to life in a global village."[12] This helps give us the skills we need to succeed in a globalized twenty-first century and to achieve our long-term educational goals. We can learn more about others, come to understand and respect foreign cultures, and see the world through different eyes. As we discussed in Chapter 1, global citizens are marked by an awareness of self and of the rest of the world. You have achieved this by reflecting on your personal and cultural identity. Global citizens make decisions based on a sense of humanity and a solid set of principles. You have gained empathy and knowledge of other cultures that have likely shaped your principles. And global citizens participate and engage actively in the world around them, especially in issues related to social justice. We hope that your experience and openness to the world will encourage you to engage actively and ethically within it.[13] In sum, study abroad gives *you* the edge.

Reentry Programming: What *You* Can Do

This chapter has explored the traditional stages of reentry and addressed some ways to meaningfully reflect on study abroad experiences. It is also important to recognize that because these themes have been identified and studied by experts, there is a wealth of programming available for you to better transition back to campus. Indeed, you may even be reading this book as an assignment for a reentry program or class at your college or university. What follows is a set of ideas and initiatives that have been designed to help students confront and overcome the disorientation that often comes with reentry.

Reentry Events

Your study abroad office may host reorientation events expressly designed to help you make the adjustment back to the home institution. Although these events may not be the first thing on your mind as you transition back to campus, we encourage you to take every advantage of them and become active in your own educational and personal journey.

Essay or Photo Contests

Study abroad offices, international studies programs, or even the program you attended may sponsor competitive essay or photo contests designed to celebrate study abroad activities. You will often find information about rules (and even prizes) posted on program, institutional, or study abroad office websites. An online web search will also bring up a number of sites offering similar contests through the *Glimpse Abroad Magazine*, organizations like TransitionsAbroad, and many others.[14]

International Program Events

You are now part of a wider community of students on campus who are connected to and celebrate world cultures, languages, art, food, history, and even politics. If you look around, you will find that there are all kinds of international programs at your institution; your recent personal experiences may give you something to share with the groups. Some of these may be academic in nature (e.g., a lecture on the crisis in Darfur), but others will be cocurricular activities outside the classroom, such as an international fashion show or banquet. Be sure to also look for activities sponsored by groups such as international student organizations, multiethnic student affairs programs, and even regional or country clubs.

Peer Counseling

You have gained an expertise and can really help orient others to what to expect during their study abroad experiences. Although you may informally advise your friends and acquaintances, many institutions sponsor organized peer mentoring programs. You should inquire about opportunities in your study abroad office first, and then seek out other offices that work with students who may need your additional insights. Imagine the possibilities of helping students to achieve some of the same joys and accomplishments you experienced while abroad—and also to avoid some of the pitfalls. Talking with fellow students also has the unexpected effect of helping you process and reflect on your own experience in a different manner.

Take a Class

You have developed such a unique perspective on the wider world: this is prime time to use that knowledge in a class related to your interests. Consider enrolling in classes dedicated to furthering your knowledge of a particular culture or language—or continue to push the boundaries of knowledge by registering for a class in a new area you would like to know more about. Remember: if you can travel around the world and succeed in foreign classrooms, you can certainly handle some new challenges back home.

Volunteer Work

You have special knowledge. Think about using this to volunteer with those in need in your community. For example, you can practice the language you learned abroad by translating in the community or tutoring younger students. Many returnees are drawn to English as a Second Language (ESL) programs, given their newfound facility of working with people from a different culture and a new understanding of the mental processes involved in learning a different language. Find community organizations that work with issues you care about.

Individual Projects

As much as we encourage you to connect with programs and activities, we also understand that readjustment is a personal process. There are all kinds of ways to remember the experience you have had, including writing poetry or prose, translating your journal into something for broader consumption, or creating a scrapbook or a photo album.

Keep in Touch

Finally, we encourage you to maintain as many contacts as possible with foreign students, host families, and friends made while abroad throughout the developmental experience. Writing letters and maintaining contact by e-mail help compensate for the sense of loss. You can still read the daily newspaper of your host country online or watch YouTube clips of your favorite shows. Remember that almost every student who returns feels a sense of loss; it is up to you to keep up the flame that you ignited while abroad.

Conclusion

There are millions of "survivors" of reentry who have made successful transitions and grown personally, academically, and professionally. And there are many good resources out there to help you cope with reentry shock. Experts talk about the several stages of reverse culture shock, including a period of reflection or decompression, allowing time to anticipate reentry difficulties, and a necessary adjustment period. In order to successfully navigate reentry, it is important, even essential, to seek out ways to share with others the challenges of reorientation. There are many family members, friends, and professionals at your school who are willing to discuss these issues with you. Seek them out and learn from them. And take time to reflect on how you have changed, and what you can bring home from your experience abroad.

Chapter Six
CONTINUING THE
EDUCATIONAL JOURNEY

This book has reflected on many important dimensions of study abroad. Now that you have successfully completed a program, where will your journey take you next? Will your foreign study experience live in your memory as a onetime opportunity, or have you embarked on a longer journey of which study abroad was just the first step?

This chapter addresses ways for students to contextualize their experiences, use their skills at intercultural competence, and strengthen their commitment to confront global issues. Many U.S. students who complete reentry surveys report that the experience helped them to "mature" and "become better problem-solvers." But often it is more challenging to purposefully integrate the experience into long-term career or life goals. This chapter offers practical approaches to translate study abroad into valuable vocational skills and a globally engaged life.

How Has the Experience Changed You?

Study abroad can be the beginning of something even more meaningful. Let's start with you: What have you gained from the study abroad experience on a personal level? Answers to this question will depend on many different factors, of course. Most students who participate in study abroad find that their interpersonal and social skills have developed through the experience. Your friends and family will notice that you have changed from your time abroad, even if you personally feel very little sense of transformation. Studies tell us that those who return from study abroad have often achieved key intrapersonal goals of cognitive and social development and maturation. And you have probably already noticed that your off-campus experience has helped make you more independent, open, and flexible.

Foreign study and travel have also provided you with a much richer understanding of your own culture and foreign cultures. Indeed, it is important to note that *you have now learned much more than many Americans ever will about living across cultures.* You have gained real insight on the values that are held dear by other populations or groups in the world. And through reflection and debriefing, you have begun to come to terms with these experiences. We are convinced that true cross-cultural understanding begins at the grassroots level, with these very types of exchanges experienced by motivated students who seek to learn more about themselves and others.

In addition, you have learned about a specific discipline or topic of study. You may have taken insightful classes on Aboriginal life in Australia, Russian politics, or Chilean culture. An Arabic language major who returns from a semester in Jordan has likely developed fluency or near-fluency in the language, as well as a deeper understanding of cultures in a comparative perspective. A geology major may have spent time abroad learning about soil composition, rock formations, or fossils in a way that would have been impossible on her home campus. A premed major may have gained valuable experience as a volunteer in a health clinic in a developing country.

Furthermore, you have directly experienced a form of integrative learning on a path to global citizenship. You have begun to make connections within overlapping communities and synthesize ideas across different disciplines of understanding. You have seen a world that, though possibly much different from where you came, shares some of the same issues and concerns that you have. Study abroad has allowed you to better understand global processes and develop the insight to "discern, not how distant these world events are from [your] immediate concerns, but how immediate concerns have threads which link [you]—[your] actions, votes, choices as consumers—to these world events."[1] In sum, you have gained the capacity to travel across not only national borders, but also across boundaries of thought, cultures, values, and beliefs.

All of these skills will help you to make an important move to the next step—integrating your experiences into your larger life story: a sense of who you are and what you stand for as a result of study abroad. In other words, your academic development through study abroad has been significant, and it helps set you apart from others. More employers in the globalizing economy seek candidates with diverse experiences, refined cognitive skills, and proficiency in intercultural competency and ethical reasoning. They also seek candidates with knowledge of human activities in the physical and natural world, including competency in the sciences and technology. You may have learned specific information about a country, but you were also able to observe the world around you. In some cases, you might also be able to use practical work or internship experience to your advantage. This concerns not just language ability, but also critical thinking, writing and verbal communication skills, quantitative analysis, literacy, teamwork, and problem solving. The next step in your educational journey is to determine how you can best use these skills and insights in furthering your education and perhaps even your career.

"Marketing" Your Knowledge

We encourage you to think strategically about how to translate study abroad experiences into a competitive edge in the job search process, career development, or preparation for graduate school. Whether overseas study takes the form of an entry on your resumé or becomes a

Figure 6.1 The Global Classroom Learning Cycle

deeper part of your personal narrative, you should not hesitate to "market" this knowledge.

Many employers value the skills that you have developed through education abroad. In his book *2006–2007 Recruiting Trends*, Phil Gardner of Michigan State University lists the following characteristics as important for employers as they consider "the total package" of any candidate:

- Communication skills, including verbal, written, and listening capabilities
- Computer/technical skills
- Leadership abilities and management skills, knowing when to lead or follow
- Teamwork and being able to work cooperatively, collaboratively, or independently as the situation requires
- Interpersonal skills: the ability to relate to others, inspire participation among others, or negotiate conflict
- Personal traits, including initiative, motivation, flexibility, adaptability, work ethic, reliability, honesty, integrity, and organizational multitasking skills[2]

Many of these characteristics can be developed or enhanced through education abroad. For instance, a large-scale survey of major employers conducted by the Council for International Educational Exchange (CIEE) found that they "do in fact value study abroad when compared to a variety of other educational experiences." The most highly valued experiences were study abroad programs of a semester or a year in length, followed by semester-long internships with relevant agencies or businesses.[3] Another recent report by the Goldman Sachs Foundation and the Asia Society begins with the proposition that "today's students must acquire a far different set of knowledge, skills, and perspectives than previous generations" if they are to live and work successfully in a complex and rapidly changing world.[4] The report concluded that there was "significant support for the belief that employers value study abroad in hiring recent college and university graduates."[5]

Thinking strategically, you can find ways to emphasize these skills in relation to your academic work and study abroad experience. We also encourage you to consider additional routes to incorporate your experience into your graduate school applications or resumé. For example, you might use relevant anecdotes in a personal essay or even during job interviews. Employers are interested in applicants' problem-solving skills, and your study abroad experience likely offered a treasure trove of ideas about embracing new challenges and solving new problems successfully.[6]

How can you get started? Visit the career office on your campus soon. Tell them about your study abroad experience and ask them for ideas about how you might incorporate the experience into longer-term career development or related opportunities. The simple process of articulating your experiences and beginning to imagine how they can serve as value-added skills for future employment is a useful exercise in itself. In addition, ask staff members at the career services and study abroad offices about summer internships and postgraduate opportunities that will take advantage of and develop your newly discovered capabilities. Talk with them about study, work, or volunteer abroad opportunities available to you in the future.

Opportunities

You can translate your study abroad experience into new opportunities. Studies tell us that students who complete education abroad programs for one full year demonstrate much more interest in further academic study and may change their major or career plans; they are also more likely to attend graduate school.[7] You are especially well prepared to take on these opportunities. What follows is a survey of some possible paths one might take in continuing the journey as a global citizen.

Graduate School

Study abroad provides an exciting foundation for graduate training. It is useful to think of potential links between study abroad at the undergraduate level and advanced degree possibilities. Some students may develop a sense of how the classes they took or experiences they had abroad translate into their longer-term plan of study, and they will know that they want to extend these in their graduate work. For example, students majoring in foreign languages who study in Italy or Kenya may have received enough training to achieve fluency in a local language and become familiar with important customs and traditions. History majors may have examined fascinating archival collections in places such as the Imperial War Museum in London, the Museo Nacional de Antropología in Mexico City, or the State Hermitage Museum in St. Petersburg, Russia. Students in the natural sciences may have received vital laboratory or field research training through study abroad, and majors in English, philosophy, or sociology may have worked directly with experts in their fields in foreign countries.

Study abroad may also have an indirect impact on your graduate school plans. We know that study abroad can effectively broaden one's horizons through encounters with different individuals, issues, controversies, or dilemmas. As a result, some students return from overseas study with newfound commitments to public service or learning more about other cultures. This inspirational effect of study abroad may lead you to consider applying for graduate training in an area you might not have anticipated three years ago. Students may discover a love for the performing arts, for example, or music, or the history of different countries. You may have been inspired by the foreign citizens or issues you encountered and seek to gain knowledge in an entirely new arena.

Graduate school opportunities typically fall into one of two categories: a master's degree (M.A.) in a specific discipline, or a doctorate (Ph.D.). Doctoral degrees are often geared to preparing students for highly advanced work in their areas of specialization, and many students who complete their Ph.D.s go into academia. Master's programs are typically geared toward the development of a proficiency that serves as an important career stepping-stone. Many universities in the United States and abroad offer advanced training, leading to a master's degree or even a Ph.D., in thematic areas that are of interest to students. Graduate programs often put a high premium on applicants' academic work and study abroad experiences. Some graduate programs, such as Ph.D. programs in political science, often have a foreign language requirement that may be fully or partially fulfilled through prior training.

Finally, you might also consider attending graduate school in a foreign country. This is becoming an increasingly attractive option for many U.S. students. European universities have begun to standardize their educational programs as part of a wider initiative known as the Bologna Process. And some foreign universities, especially in northern Europe and Scandinavia, have begun to develop graduate programs geared directly toward U.S. students and taught in English. According to one survey, in

2008 there were more than 900 degree programs at universities in the Netherlands and more than 450 master's programs in Sweden where the entire curriculum was conducted in English.[8]

Many graduate programs offer financial aid, scholarships, assistant-ships, and fellowships that will help defray the costs of education. In some situations fellowships may pay the entire costs of your tuition and fees for graduate schooling as well as offer you a monthly stipend simply to attend their program. Teaching or research assistantships can involve part-time work in academic programs in exchange for similar benefits. So, if you are considering applying to graduate programs after commence-ment, or even if this is an eventuality years after graduation, be sure to consult with professors and staff members at your campus about the requirements and process.

Grants for Study Abroad

There are many opportunities for recent college graduates to obtain financial support in the form of grants for returning overseas. Many of these grants are directed to the support of research in foreign countries and may apply to any discipline; some are linked to specific graduate degree programs. Examples include the Carnegie Endowment for Inter-national Peace's Junior Fellowship program, the Andrew W. Mellon Fel-lowship in the Humanities, the Rhodes Scholarship, the British Marshall Scholarship, and the National Science Foundation Graduate Fellowship. Yet others provide broader training opportunities. The more one explores the options for funding for education, research, and study abroad, the more fascinating the possibilities.

The following three examples illustrate the range of grant opportu-nities to return overseas. First, the Woodrow Wilson Foundation sponsors internship and scholarship programs related to career tracks in U.S. gov-ernment agencies. Some of these scholarships will support several years' worth of study and include summer institutes and internships. Second, the German Academic Exchange Service (DAAD) is another major funding agency that provides students and teachers the opportunity to take classes abroad in Germany. DAAD provides supplemental funds for graduate studies in natural science, business, law, medicine, and the social sciences. It also funds special intensive language study grants. Third, the National Security Education Program (NSEP) provides millions of dol-lars in grants for U.S. graduate students to pursue advanced training in select area and language study. NSEP Boren Graduate Fellowships support the study of languages, cultures, and world regions that are critical to U.S. national security but less frequently studied.[9] These and other grant opportunities are available to competitive applicants. Your study abroad experience framed around a clear academic focus may give you the edge you need to obtain these grants.

International Careers

Most college students will begin full-time employment after graduation. Through planning you may be able to secure a job that links you to the world. Examples of career opportunities that relate directly to global understanding can be found in international finance and banking, the travel industry, computer programming or Internet-based technologies, the energy sector, or manufacturing. *In other words, today it is hard to find employment opportunities that do not offer some sort of global connection.*

This discussion is divided into two general categories: nonprofit organizations and the corporate sector. The next stop for some students who have studied abroad may be work in a nonprofit organization like the World Wildlife Fund. For others, career development will involve work in a for-profit organization such as a multinational corporation. Regardless of the path you choose, though, we are convinced that the future for students who participate in study abroad can be exciting and fulfilling.

Nonprofit Organizations

Many students consider work in the nonprofit sector after graduation. Nonprofits, also referred to as nongovernmental organizations (NGOs), are foundations, charities, or volunteer organizations that provide needed services. Fortunately, nonprofits are often looking for entry-level professionals who share the commitment of their organization or have understanding of their mission in the world. Study abroad provides you with a special entrée to such opportunities. One may consider a career working in the nonprofit sector with organizations that specialize in international affairs, global issues, international travel, or even study abroad. There are literally thousands of opportunities related to service and international experiences, and some of them listed in the Resources section of this book may help you get started.

As with any search for employment, you may find that the perfect nonprofit organization that fits your interests does not hire dozens of new, eager college graduates for instant careers in service. But many nonprofits have enticing internship programs that allow one to get a "foot in the door." Take the Carter Center as an example. This is a nonprofit organization established by former president Jimmy Carter, based in Atlanta and associated with Emory University. Its primary missions are to promote peaceful settlement of enduring conflicts and rivalries and to promote control and eradication of diseases around the world. Center staff members are involved in activities including country research, mediation of disputes, election monitoring, and strategic analysis. The Carter Center Internship Program offers opportunities for recent graduates to work at the institute part-time, unpaid, for several months in order to test opportunities. Another example, the Chicago Council on Foreign Relations, offers a similar internship program for recent graduates to link directly with important issues in foreign affairs. These are but two of many possible internship opportunities that may enable you to get started on a career in the nonprofit sector.

In addition, there are many different kinds of work or volunteer opportunities that one might consider; some may even be a virtual extension of the study abroad experience. Thousands of charity and volunteer organizations around the world would welcome help—especially from young people who have already developed cross-cultural awareness and valuable skills. NGOs like Catholic Relief Service, Greenpeace, the World Wildlife Fund, and Amnesty International are always looking for volunteers. Some of the programs sponsored by these organizations are also based in foreign countries (see Resources).

Multinational Corporations

Working for a multinational corporation offers another path to combine your study abroad experience and undergraduate training with a commitment to global engagement. Multinational corporations are major companies that have a headquarters operation in one country and subsidiaries in one or more other countries. These include tens of thousands of firms: banks, agricultural groups, energy companies, fashion designers, manufacturers, and many other businesses. While you may not have considered working for a large corporation as a career path, the reality today is that a significant percentage of college graduates do end up working for some period in this type of company. Once again, the skills you have developed through study abroad may make you uniquely suited to embrace these types of employment opportunities after graduation. It is no surprise in this era of globalization that there are ever more opportunities in multinational corporations—and ever more of them in which to find opportunities.

Multinational corporations typically have headquarters in advanced industrialized countries and branches and subsidiaries around the world. The Procter & Gamble Company, for example, has a home in Cincinnati, Ohio, but tens of thousands of its employees work around the United States and in several foreign countries. Starbucks Corporation has offices in Seattle, Washington, but branches and subsidiaries in North America, Latin America, and even Russia. H&M is a European fashion design and merchandising company that was founded in Sweden and now has branches throughout Europe and North America. Sony is a massive multinational company with global headquarters in Japan and subsidiaries throughout Asia, Europe, Latin America, Africa, and North America. Thousands of other companies are vibrant organizations that employ young people in fascinating careers—from management and finance to customer service to product research and merchandising.[10]

Work with multinational corporations may offer you future travel or educational opportunities. For example, some corporations pay for their employees to take graduate classes or offer other incentives. They may also offer opportunities for foreign work excursions and, sometimes, postings in foreign countries. And they will most likely allow you to work with people from backgrounds different from your own, providing new opportunities for cross-cultural learning. Your skills in language training, cross-cultural communication, and critical thinking may help you gain access to this world. Ultimately, there is no limit to where your career may take you.

Teaching

Study abroad provides unique encounters with the world, and teaching seems a natural fit for some students who have traveled abroad. Many people are first drawn to education abroad programs by their curiosity about the world and interest in learning more about other peoples and cultures. Indeed, this same disposition may fit well with a career in teaching, which can provide unique and satisfying opportunities to share knowledge (and love of the world or select countries and cultures) with others. Furthermore, teaching careers often feature exciting professional development opportunities including international travel and study.

Teaching opportunities abound. Indeed, short-term teaching postings abroad are popular options for paid or inexpensive long-term stays overseas. Considerable cultural immersion is possible, especially if you have some knowledge of foreign languages. In some cases, proficiency in the language of the host country may be required for these postings, but in others it is not.

The "traditional" path for teaching in the United States is training to work in primary or secondary education. Students prepare for this by completing a bachelor's degree (in nearly any field) along with a master's degree in teaching or equivalent teaching certification. Returnees from study abroad may feel compelled to develop teaching skills related to a specific discipline such as foreign languages. Others may be motivated by study abroad to specialize in international relations or history and teach social studies at the secondary level. Those exposed to science, art, or music programs through study abroad may translate their experiences into specialized teaching at the primary or secondary level.

Corbin Boisvert, Wooster in Chiang Mai, Thailand

There are also exciting options for teaching that do not necessarily involve embarking on a lifelong career. For example, the Teach for America and the Volunteers in Service to America (AmeriCorps VISTA) programs offer opportunities for teacher training that typically require one- to two-year commitments. Teach for America is one of the fastest growing teaching and service programs in the United States today. The program matches aspiring recent college graduates with teaching apprentice opportunities elsewhere in the country. Postings are often in inner-city or underresourced school systems around the United States, and the Teach for America volunteers gain a deep sense of appreciation for others.[11] The AmeriCorps VISTA program offers selected college graduates opportunities to become involved in teaching and community organizing initiatives in the United States. Both programs have an admirable record of public service and celebrate the achievements of their members and alumni.[12]

In addition, fellowship and scholarship opportunities are available to sponsor U.S. college graduates to teach select subjects or English as a foreign language abroad. The J. William Fulbright Fellowship program is one of the most prestigious and is sponsored by the U.S. Department of State and the U.S. Congress. The Fulbright program was first established in 1946 by Congress to "enable the government of the United States to increase mutual understanding between the people of the United States and the people of other countries." Each year, 700 Fulbright postgraduate scholarships are awarded to U.S. citizens who are assigned to teach abroad in elementary and secondary schools.[13]

Short-term opportunities for teaching English abroad also appeal to some graduates with prior overseas study experience. For example, the Japan Exchange and Teaching (JET) Program provides opportunities for college graduates from around the world to travel to Japan and teach classes on English language or culture. The JET program is a nonprofit exchange that began over twenty years ago with an orientation toward grassroots connections to promote cross-cultural understanding. With globalization and the rising importance of Asia for the global economy, the program has thrived and now draws participants from more than forty countries.[14] Other programs for teaching English as a second language sponsor U.S. students who seek to spend one or more years abroad teaching in a foreign country. Some of these programs may require you to attain certification through short courses offered at many U.S. universities. Be sure to research basic requirements of such programs; much of this information is available online. We encourage you to approach thinking about where to teach English abroad the same way you did study abroad; consider your own personal motivations and then where you would like to teach and why. And remember that you will likely need a special type of visa that allows you to work, volunteer, intern, or do research in a foreign country through these programs.

Finally, students may consider academic careers in higher education. This path to teaching in the United States or abroad is open to highly motivated students. College graduates typically pursue a master's or doctoral degree in order to gain necessary certification for employment. As these students approach graduation from their degree programs, they may explore teaching opportunities at colleges and universities in the United States or abroad. Today there are more and more posted opportunities for such employment at foreign universities that seek to diversify their faculties by hosting U.S. instructors for short-term or even long-term employment.

Public Service

Many students who participate in study abroad programs care about the interests and concerns of others. This special combination of qualities—a commitment to service coupled with curiosity about the world around you and the capacity to cross cultures and boundaries—is characteristic of "global citizens." Your desire to address global issues and your ability to work with colleagues from different cultures may make you particularly well suited to explore careers in public service. For example, returnees may build on and promote their experiences in order to explore government opportunities around the United States or the world. Students who have traveled extensively and gained deep insight may be fascinated by the potential for a career in the Department of State Foreign Service Officer corps or the Department of Commerce or the National Transportation Safety Board.

The Peace Corps

The Peace Corps is one of the highest-profile public service programs sponsored by the U.S. government for work in a foreign country. Peace Corps volunteers are college graduates who commit to a term of service of two years in a foreign country. The work of the Peace Corps ranges from public health programs to education and social welfare, and volunteers typically work in rural areas of developing countries. The Peace Corps provides you with direct, hands-on field experience that can change your life. Indeed, tens of thousands of Americans who have participated in the program since its inception in the 1960s have gone on to productive lives as engaged global citizens. Ask around and you might find a former volunteer living and working in your community today. In addition, the Peace Corps offers exciting professional development opportunities. The Peace Corps Master's International Program (MIP) combines field service with a master's degree program.[15] For more information on this and similar volunteer programs, see the Resources.

The U.S. Department of State and the Foreign Service

The U.S. Department of State, or State Department, is the main arm of diplomacy for the U.S. government. The department's staff includes tens of thousands of civilian employees dedicated to foreign policy making, from country and issue experts to translators and immigration policy specialists. The main headquarters for the State Department is in Washington, D.C., but it also coordinates staff in hundreds of embassies, consulates, and mission offices around the world. This is one of many U.S. government agencies that regularly hires young and talented college graduates and features an intriguing internship program.

The Foreign Service Officer (FSO) corps is an elite branch of the State Department that includes about 3,500 diplomats posted in Washington or U.S. embassies, consulates, and missions around the world. FSOs are selected through a screening process that involves taking challenging written and oral examinations; those selected receive extensive training in foreign cultures and languages. FSOs then embark on exciting diplomatic careers that can involve regular foreign travel, cross-cultural interaction, and extensive learning about global affairs. Some FSOs will go on to become top experts on foreign policy for the president of the United States, executives at policy research institutes, and even ambassadors.[16]

According to the State Department, students may prepare for careers in diplomacy by majoring in almost any discipline and striving for academic excellence. Foreign language fluency and cross-cultural understanding are essential qualities for FSOs. Indeed, developing the characteristics emphasized in this book will help strengthen your preparation for a career in diplomacy.

International Governmental Organizations

There are hundreds of major international governmental organizations (IGOs) active in global affairs today. IGOs are transnational institutions that have country governments as members. The most prominent example of an IGO is the United Nations. The United Nations employs more than 50,000 staff members worldwide, working in administrative posts, economics, electronic data processing, finance, language-related work, legal affairs (primarily international law), research-oriented work, public information, statistics, and social development. Because the UN is a very large organization, it regularly hires employees through a routine recruitment and application process that can include language examinations. The UN also sponsors career development through its junior professional and professional tracks. Furthermore, dozens of agencies and affiliated organizations such as the UN World Food Program, the UN Children's Fund (UNICEF), the UN Commission on Human Rights (UNCHR), and the UN Development Programme (UNDP) recruit new employees for projects and offices around the world.

The United Nations may be the most prominent example of an IGO, but there are literally hundreds of other organizations that employ global citizens. Examples include the World Trade Organization (WTO), headquartered in Geneva, Switzerland. The WTO is the world's foremost organization devoted to the promotion of liberalized trade and the removal of tariff and nontariff barriers to trade around the world. The WTO is thus a combination of an economic watchdog organization and an international court for the nonviolent settlement of trade disputes. A very different type of IGO is the International Monetary Fund (IMF). Headquartered in Washington, D.C., and with affiliate offices all over the world, the IMF is dedicated to promoting economic development and monetary and fiscal policy coordination. The IMF employs specialists in communications, economics, financial services, languages, and information technology. Its activities range from supporting countries facing balance-of-payments problems to the global fight against terrorism.

Conclusion

In this chapter, we have encouraged you to think about ways to keep your overseas study experience alive in terms of your educational and career development. Many students who return from study abroad begin imagining ways to return or learn more about specific countries or regions. They may seek research or teaching grants that allow them to travel overseas again after graduation. Others will turn their foreign language skills into marketing tools for jobs in multinational corporations. Some students will be so inspired by experiences abroad that they will consider entirely different life paths than ever before. In essence, this chapter is about how you can recalibrate your life in the wake of successful and exciting experiences abroad.

It is time now to embrace this possibility and take action. By pushing yourself to explore exciting new educational or career opportunities, you will continue to grow. The world is becoming a smaller place—borders are blurring, and we are all becoming global citizens. You have an opportunity through study abroad to get ahead of the curve by becoming an informed and engaged citizen of the world.[17] Finally, regardless of your immediate plans, it is important to remember that study abroad can be the beginning of an exciting, lifelong journey of discovery. The more education and cross-cultural experiences you attain, the more opportunities you will likely find for fulfilling work, travel, or study abroad. This is a great time in your life to embrace these challenges and take risks. Go ahead, explore!

WORKSHEETS

The following worksheets are derived from the learning cycle and learning dimensions models presented in *The Global Classroom: An Essential Guide to Study Abroad*. These worksheets may be employed in predeparture, orientation, and reorientation workshops or offered as part of an online orientation program. In workshop settings, advisers and faculty might encourage students to work in groups on the worksheets. They may also assist individual students as they prepare for, participate in, and return from a study abroad experience. In all cases, students should think about and discuss these questions as they pertain to each dimension of the global classroom and academic objectives.

Worksheet 1: Before You Go—Dimensions of the Global Classroom Experience

Most discussions of study abroad begin with where you want to go. But a much more fascinating place to start this dialogue is with *why* you want to study abroad. Indeed, the global classroom starts with you. Learning more about who you are may be the key to understanding your motivations in relation to the academic objectives of the experience. In *The Global Classroom*, we suggest four major dimensions of the global classroom experience: personal identity, cultural identity, vocational development, and global citizenship (see Figure W.1). These dimensions may offer a useful guide for framing your journey to know more about yourself, others, and the world.

Figure W.1   Dimensions of the Global Classroom

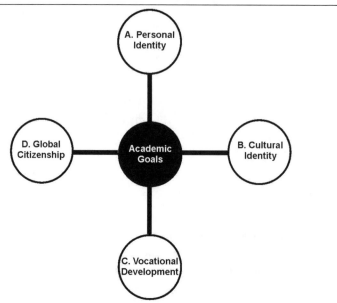

WORKSHEET 1
BEFORE YOU GO—DIMENSIONS OF THE GLOBAL CLASSROOM

A. Personal Identity

Why do you want to study abroad?

What do you hope to gain from the experience on a personal level?

Do you consider yourself to be open-minded? Optimistic or pessimistic? Explain.

What worries or concerns do you have about logistics or adaptation during your experience abroad?

Are you flexible? Do you adapt easily to new circumstances? Explain.

Are you ready to meet new people and explore a new and different environment? How do you plan to do this while you are abroad?

B. *Cultural Identity*

How might you describe your own culture?

Would you say that you have a single or multiple cultural identities? Explain.

How would you explain your culture to others?

How do you represent your home country, its culture, its government, its traditions, its way of life?

Are you ready to adapt to a new culture? How do you plan to do this while you are abroad?

C. Vocational Development

What sort of learning experiences do you want to have?

What do you want to learn about a particular culture or language?

How do you picture yourself using this experience when you return? At your home institution? Professionally?

Do you want to learn or perfect a language other than your native language?

What is the best kind of instruction and learning environment for you: a traditional classroom or experiential activities?

D. Global Citizenship

Do you identify yourself as someone who can make a difference in the world? Explain.

What sort of global issues interest you? Are you concerned about health, environmental, social justice, or other global issues?

Do you relate well to others? Explain.

How do you interact with people of backgrounds different from yours?

What do you know about other countries, regions, or cultures of the world?

Why are you curious about other regions, countries, or cultures of the world?

Have you traveled, studied, or lived abroad before? If so, what was your experience like?

How will you explain your culture and background to others?

Worksheet 2: Selecting the Right Program for You

Choosing the program that is the best fit for you is a key step to ensuring a meaningful, beneficial learning experience abroad. In Chapter 2 we review ways that you can familiarize yourself with the options available to you in relation to your school's policies on study abroad and requirements for graduation. Be sure to take the time necessary to ask questions about the program and think about the many factors involved—from the practical aspects of program duration, location, model, or requirements to your academic and personal goals and specific needs. Remember that selecting the right study abroad program for you may be the key to a memorable, challenging, and rewarding experience.

When considering the following questions, be sure to reflect on all four dimensions of the global classroom experience: personal identity, cultural identity, vocational training, and global citizenship.

WORKSHEET 2
SELECTING THE RIGHT PROGRAM FOR YOU

A. Program Paradigms and Characteristics

Which of the following programs are you considering: direct enrollment, an institutionally run program, an institution-sponsored exchange, or a program provider? Why?

Which of the following features do you seek in a program: courses with other Americans, courses at a local university, courses taught by local faculty, courses taught by U.S. professors, field research, internship, or service learning? Why are these important to you?

What is the length of the program you are considering? Why did you choose this program length? In your opinion, what are the advantages and disadvantages of this period of study?

What are your housing options through this program? What are the educational advantages and disadvantages of your preference for housing?

B. Program Location

What is the location of the program you are considering? Why do you seek to study in this location?

What are the educational advantages and disadvantages of this location or region in particular?

Is the program localized in a single location or is it a traveling program? Why did you choose one of these options over the other?

C. Learning Environment

What courses should you take before you go to best prepare yourself for the experience? Do you feel prepared to attend this program?

What is the native language where you will be studying? In what languages will classes be taught?

Are there structured opportunities for cultural or experiential learning? Does the program offer study in a local university, internships or volunteering for academic credit, or field study?

How do you plan on actively reflecting on your experience? Will the program guide you in any way?

Will you be taking classes with local students, other international students, or Americans? What are the advantages and disadvantages of this option?

D. Logistics and Support

How much on-site support do you need or want?

What type of in-country orientation is provided? Will you have support for choosing classes, registering, integrating into the community, getting around the city?

What sorts of activities exist to help you integrate into the host community and meet locals?

How do you plan on getting the information you need to manage your expectations about the program? With whom will you discuss your plans?

Worksheet 3: Engaging with Your Experience Through Critical Reflection

Getting the most out of your experience means taking every opportunity for critical reflection about yourself and your place in your host culture and in the world. As you begin to have powerful experiences abroad, we would encourage you to chronicle them, reflecting on all four dimensions of your learning experience: your personal identity, your cultural identity, vocational and skills learning, and global citizenship.

For this exercise, choose one of the suggested formats to answer each set of questions.

WORKSHEET 3
ENGAGING WITH YOUR EXPERIENCE THROUGH
CRITICAL REFLECTION

Suggested Formats for Critical Reflection

Journaling. First and foremost, journaling is a means of private and deliberate reflection that allows you to express, organize, and record your thoughts and feelings and to maintain a certain awareness about your experience. As you put your ideas and emotions into perspective, you are also connecting with the world around you through observations and reflections. Many students keep daily journal entries and take time to record their thoughts and experiences while they are fresh.

Blogging. Blogging has become a popular medium for today's student. Given the interactive nature of blogging, it can offer a social support system as well as an opportunity for internal reflection. Blogs provide a forum for sharing emotions and thoughts, and discussing challenging events in a way unlike face-to-face communication. Blogs can help you create a network with other students, allow you to keep friends and family at home updated on your experiences and well-being, or even act as a call for help for students in distress. Make sure that what you write about reflects *you*: your voice, your experience, your personality. There are many great online resources for inspiration and tips about blogging.

Writing Letters or E-Mails Home. We typically think of critical reflection occurring in journals or homework assignments, but it can take on many forms. The note you write to yourself on a café napkin, the e-mail you write to a friend back home, or a letter to your family all constitute exercises of active reflection. Your reflections might include a description of what you did on a certain day, what you saw at a museum, or what you had for dinner, or they might touch on deeper emotions and feelings.

Being a Cultural Ethnographer. Adopt an ethnographic research method in your writing, like the O.D.I.S. (Observe, Describe, Interpret, Suspend Judgment) or D.I.E. (Description, Interpretation, Evaluation) method. They will guide your reflection, helping you become more culturally aware and gain critical observation skills. In these exercises of active reflection, you should first observe verbal and nonverbal cues. Then, mentally describe to yourself what is happening, or what you see, or how you feel. Next, create various interpretations based on your personal worldview to help yourself make sense of the observations and descriptions. Finally, put yourself in your hosts' shoes to attempt to understand them and yourself: you might acknowledge your discomfort with an unfamiliar situation, decide to observe similar events, consult others for feedback, or respect differences and defer judgment.

Writing a Column for Your School Newspaper. Now that you have spent a few weeks or months in your host culture, you are certainly aware of the benefits of study abroad. Share your transformative experiences with your friends and classmates back home. Pick a topic or event that has profoundly interested you and write about it. Remember the famous "who, what, when, where, why, and how" of journalism, keep it interesting and concise, and stay on topic. Consider your classmates' perspective and write about something that interests both you and them!

Questions for Reflection

A. Personal Identity

What have you experienced or seen that has caused you to reflect on your personal identity?

You know about the different stages of culture shock and cultural adaptation. Tell about when you have experienced some of the stages: Honeymoon Stage, Culture Stress/Shock, Integration, Adaptation, and Acceptance.

What are your "coping mechanisms" when you feel anxious, sad, or "culture shocked"?

Do you feel that your personal identity, your worldviews, your opinions, or your beliefs have been affected or are being affected by your time abroad?

B. Cultural Identity

What have you experienced or seen that has caused you to reflect on your cultural identity, or on the culture of your hosts?

What are the most significant differences between your home culture and your host culture? How about similarities?

Have you had any conversations or encounters with your hosts where you have discussed your differences or similarities, in a general sense?

Do you think that your hosts have any generalizations or stereotypes about your cultural identity? Do you find that you have any about theirs?

Tell about a time when you think you might have experienced "culture shock." How did you feel? Why do you think this occurred?

Has there been a time when you have noticed your own "cultural conditioning" or your personal cultural norms that have interfered with those of your hosts? What did you do to adjust?

Has there been a time when you felt that you were acting in your role as a cultural "ambassador" for your home country? Tell about it.

C. Vocational Development

What new skills have you learned since you have been on-site?

Have you thought about how these new skills will transfer once you are home? Give some examples.

If you are learning a new language, tell about a time when you noticed improvement in your language skills. Tell about a time when you have felt challenged to communicate effectively.

How have your predeparture experiences—classes you took, people you talked to—influenced your academic and vocational development on-site?

D. Global Citizenship

Do you feel that you are becoming more aware of the world around you? How?

How do you feel when you have had to "cross cultures" or interact in different cultural contexts or communities? Tell about a time when you have had to do this.

Have you ever had difficulty communicating across cultures? What have been some surprising, funny, or even awkward encounters? What have you learned from these experiences?

What have you experienced or seen that has caused you to reflect on your role as a citizen of the world?

Worksheet 4: When You Return—
Dimensions of the Global Classroom

Welcome home! You have completed a rewarding study abroad program. It may seem like the world has opened up to you and there are unlimited new opportunities. But simply going abroad may not guarantee the realization of intercultural competency and personal development. Indeed, research shows that by talking about and reflecting on your experiences *after* returning home, you can gain a much deeper perspective. Many students who return from abroad believe the experience helped them; they gained maturity, independence, and some problem-solving skills. Yet many also say it is difficult to contextualize exactly how the experience will fit into long-term education, career, or life goals.

Reentry is a very important part of your educational journey. In *The Global Classroom*, we emphasize a link between this phase and your academic development core (see Figure W.2). Ultimately, this phase of your journey is about ways to see study abroad as a *beginning*, not an end in itself.

Figure W.2   Dimensions of the Global Classroom

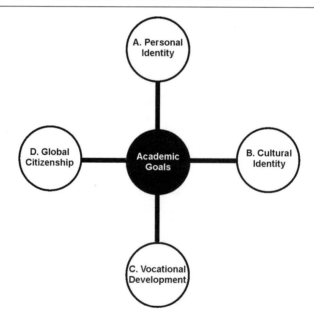

WORKSHEET 4
WHEN YOU RETURN—DIMENSIONS OF THE GLOBAL CLASSROOM

A. *Personal Identity*

Were you able to adapt to the new environment abroad?

Did your values, beliefs, or worldviews change?

How did you feel when you transitioned into life in your host country?

How did you feel when you transitioned back into life at home?

Did you experience "culture shock"? If so, how did you deal with it?

What are some of your challenges and how do you deal with them?

Did you adapt your original "expectations" or goals throughout your experience?

B. Cultural Identity

How would you describe your cultural identity now? Would you say you have one or many cultural identities?

Do you feel that you adapted well to your host culture? What hurdles did you have and how did you overcome them?

Do you feel that any of your cultural or political views about your home country have changed?

Did you learn anything new about your own culture? Or do you feel differently about it?

How did you do as an ambassador for your culture? Did you successfully explain your culture to others?

C. Vocational Development

What did you learn in the classroom in relation to your major or minor?

What did you learn about new topics?

How do you plan to use your experience back at your home institution? Professionally?

Did you improve speaking, reading, or writing in a foreign language? Were you able to communicate effectively in the language?

Do you plan on continuing study in the foreign language you learned abroad?

What other skills have you learned?

D. Global Citizenship

Do you feel that you interacted well with others? How has this experienced helped you prepare for future cross-cultural experiences?

Do you feel more globally engaged? Do you feel more apt to participate in activities that deal with global issues?

Do you feel more or less curious about other countries of the world now?

How do you feel about your role in the world now?

How do you feel interacting with your hosts? Did you experience challenges—or successes—in communicating with others?

Resources

Here we present a comprehensive list of resources that may help you plan and learn more about study abroad. We provide detailed information on websites, online resources, and print resources that will allow you to explore dimensions of your educational journey in greater detail. As always, these lists are not meant as endorsements of any particular program or website content, but rather suggestions for references we find helpful.

Online Resources for Study Abroad and International Travel

International Education and Study Abroad

American Council on Education's Center for International Initiatives:
www.acenet.edu/Content/NavigationMenu/ProgramsServices/cii/index.htm
Programs, discussions, and toolkits for internationalization of U.S. campuses. Resources for articles, policies, and studies on international education.

Association of International Education Administrators:
www.aieaworld.org
A professional membership association for international education institutional leaders that provides a forum for dialogue and information sharing, public policy advocacy, and promoting international education at institutes of higher education.

Center for Global Education:

www.globaled.us

> An online resource center promoting international education and cross-cultural learning through a variety of projects and resources, including:

> Global Scholars (for-fee online course taking you through the study abroad experience before departure, on-site, and upon return): http://global scholar.us/

> Research Online (bibliographies and abstracts about study abroad research): http://globaled.us/ro/

> Center for Global Education Resources for Study Abroad: http://globaled.us/rfsa/

> AllAbroad (resource website for students, parents, faculty, and administrators in real-life question-and-answer format): http://allabroad.us/about.php

> Safety Abroad First—Educational Travel Information (SAFETI) Clearinghouse (information on health and safety in the development and implementation of study abroad programs, including links to U.S. government organizations, higher education associations, a program audit checklist, resources for program administrators, and information about workshops): http://globaled.us/safeti/

> Center for Global Education Study Abroad Student Handbook (handbook covering all aspects of study abroad from program research to reentry; see description below): http://studentsabroad.com/

> Project for Learning in the United States (PLUS) (resources and initiatives for international students in the United States): http://globaled.us/plus/

Forum on Education Abroad:

www.forumea.org

> A membership organization serving the field of study abroad through educational programming for professionals, creation of standards of good practice, and support for research initiatives.

Frontiers: The Interdisciplinary Journal of Study Abroad

www.frontiersjournal.com

> An interdisciplinary and academic journal featuring research on study abroad; published by the Forum on Education Abroad.

IES Model Assessment Practice:

www.iesabroad.org/IES/Advisors_and_Faculty/iesMap.html

> An educational tool for designing and evaluating study abroad programs. The guidelines were developed through extensive site visits and data analyses of components of both "hybrid" and "direct enrollment" study abroad programs.

Institute for International Education:

www.iie.org

> A nonprofit membership organization supporting programs and initiatives in international education. In addition to providing resources about international education, IIE manages over 250 programs and publishes the "Open Doors Report on International Educational Exchange," a comprehensive summary of data on international students in the United States and U.S. students abroad. It also manages a number of scholarship and funding programs for international education.

Intercultural Press:

www.interculturalpress.com

> A publishing house focusing on intercultural issues and research.

International Association of Universities Database on Higher Education Systems:

www.unesco.org/iau/onlinedatabases/index.html

> A database providing information on higher education systems in over 180 countries and territories.

NAFSA: Association of International Educators:

www.nafsa.org

> A professional membership organization that promotes international education and provides professional development opportunities through conferences, online forums and resources, online and print publications, awards, and grants.

Online Study Abroad Guides, Handbooks, Databases, and Blogs

AbroadView:

www.abroadview.org

> A print and online journal providing resources and articles about study abroad for students, alumni, faculty, advisers, and parents. Topics include predeparture and returnee issues, academics and research, fellowships and careers, real-life stories, and sustainable and ethical study abroad.

Café Abroad:

www.cafeabroad.com

> An online network serving students and study abroad offices with electronic and print magazines and city guides.

Center for Global Education Study Abroad Student Handbook:

http://studentsabroad.com/

> Handbook covering program research and selection, financing study abroad, predeparture planning, legal considerations, housing, packing, communication

while abroad, expectation management, health and safety considerations, insurance coverage, risk management, culture shock, and reentry.

Council on International Educational Exchange Knowledge Series:

www.ciee.org/program_resources/knowledge.aspx

Downloadable brochures on various topics pertaining to study abroad, such as health, safety, reentry, risk management, food, identity, communication, and ambassadorship. The series addresses special concerns for parents, women, and students with disabilities.

Glimpse Abroad:

www.glimpse.org

An extensive library of articles written by students, including country-specific information, cultural topics, adjustment issues, and editorials. Features include blogs, an online store, a newsletter, and a directory of international programs. Glimpse and National Geographic cosponsor a correspondents' program for students interested in regular written submissions from abroad.

GoAbroad.com:

www.goabroad.com

Travel guides, program directories, and other resources for study, volunteer, intern, work, and teaching opportunities abroad.

IIEPassport:

www.iiepassport.com

A program directory, country and program feature articles, news articles, and informational resources for students and advisers, from the Institute of International Education.

NAFSA Student Accounts About Studying Abroad:

www.nafsa.org/students.sec/studying_abroad_from/student_accounts_gathered

Personal accounts from students about their study abroad experiences. The website also links to other online resources for study abroad.

SAFETI Adaptation of Peace Corps Resources:

www.globaled.us/peacecorps/

Handbooks and worksheets covering predeparture health training, risk and crisis management, and personal safety and awareness.

StudyAbroad.com:

www.studyabroad.com

A study, internship, and volunteer abroad program database, study abroad handbook, and information about financial aid and scholarships for off-campus study. StudyAbroad.com also hosts a blog featuring current study abroad participants.

Transitions Abroad:

www.transitionsabroad.com

An online magazine, articles, and resources for study and work abroad, cultural travel, volunteering, and international living. A wide variety of articles are written by and for students in the online webzine.

U.S. Department of State Guide for Study Abroad:

http://studentsabroad.state.gov/

Travel documents, maps, health considerations, emergency preparedness, U.S. embassies, and other concerns for U.S. students abroad. Includes links to websites about cultural exchanges, international careers, and the Fulbright program.

U.S. Department of State Tips for Studying Abroad:

http://travel.state.gov/travel/living/studying/studying_1238.html

Tips for students, women traveling alone, and for spring break travel, including advice on preparation and travel documents.

What's up with Culture?

www.pacific.edu/sis/culture/

A step-by-step online cultural training resource for study abroad (predeparture and reentry), including worksheets and activities.

Health and Safety

American College Health Association:

www.acha.org

A professional organization advocating for college and university health programs and standards.

Association for Safe International Road Travel:

www.asirt.org

Road travel reports including road conditions, transportation options, regulations, and statistics. Tips for road travel safety and best practices. The website features a special section on study abroad.

Centers for Disease Control and Prevention:

www.cdc.gov

A public health agency working under the Department of Health and Human Services of the U.S. government. The "Travelers' Health" section of the website provides information by destination and for specific groups traveling abroad. Topics include vaccinations, specific risks and diseases, mosquito and tick protection, food and water, illness and injury, and other resources and links. The website includes up-to-date warnings and announcements for travelers.

EmbassyWorld:

www.embassyworld.com

> Database of embassy websites around the world.

Facts on Tap:

www.factsontap.org

> Facts, advice, and resources about drinking and drug abuse for students and parents, from the nonprofit provider of substance abuse treatment, Phoenix House, in affiliation with the American Council for Drug Education and the Center on Addiction and the Family.

Healthy Minds:

www.healthyminds.org

> The American Psychiatric Association's resource website with links and fact sheets for mental health issues.

International Association for Medical Assistance to Travelers:

www.iamat.org/

> A nonprofit membership organization providing advice about health risks, diseases, and immunization requirements for foreign countries, with online resources for nonmembers.

International Society of Travel Medicine:

www.istm.org

> ISTM promotes travel health through education, the development of guidelines, and the promotion of research. The website hosts a travel clinic directory and links to health-related sites for nonmembers.

Office of Global Health:

www.globalhealth.gov

> A Department of Health and Human Services office representing the U.S. government internationally in affairs concerning international and refugee health. The website provides information on world health issues by country and topic, in addition to international health regulations.

The Travel Clinic by Dr. Mark Wise:

www.drwisetravel.com

> A family doctor provides general information on predeparture health preparations, vaccinations, first-aid kits, common travel health concerns, reentry health concerns, information for travelers with special health issues, women's issues, along with many useful links.

Travel Health Online:

www.tripprep.com

> Tips for healthy travel by a private travel health organization organized by destination and by health issue. The site also features a travel medicine provider database.

ULifeline:

www.ulifeline.com

> An online resource center for college mental health with fact sheets on common mental health issues for college students as well as many useful links.

U.S. Department of State's Bureau of Consular Affairs:

www.travel.state.gov

> Visa and passport information, travel warnings, services for U.S. citizens abroad, information on embassies and consulates in foreign countries. Students can also register with U.S. embassies abroad: https://travelregistration .state.gov/ibrs/ui/

World Health Organization:

www.who.int

> WHO is the directing and coordinating health agency of the United Nations. The website provides information on world health by country and by topic, in addition to online and print publications.

Students with Special Needs

Mobility International USA:

www.miusa.org

> An organization helping people with disabilities around the world travel and study internationally through online resources about programs, projects, funding, specific concerns, and success stories. In addition to online features the website includes searchable databases for disability organizations and exchange programs.

The University of Minnesota Learning Abroad Center:

www.umabroad.umn.edu/access

> Resources for students and professionals including website links, success stories, checklists for preparing to study abroad, information about access at overseas sites, and predeparture considerations.

Information for Underrepresented Students

Access International Education: Resources for Underrepresented Groups in International Education:

www.ucis.pitt.edu/aie/

> A website of resource lists, links, and guidebooks for students, parents, administrators, and researchers, hosted by the University Center for International Studies at the University of Pittsburgh. The center also publishes online "The World Is in Your Hands: African-Americans Speak Out and

Share Their International Experiences," where African-American students respond to survey questions about their experiences abroad: www.ucis.pitt .edu/aie/resources/TWIIYH.pdf.

"Diversity Issues in Study Abroad":

www.brown.edu/Administration/OIP/pdf_docs/diversity_st_abroad01.pdf

In this publication of the Office of International Programs at Brown University, students talk about their experiences in various countries.

Journeywoman:

www.journeywoman.com

Suggestions on shopping, restaurants, clothing, guidebooks, and many other articles and personal stories directed toward women travelers. The website offers to put women travelers in contact with each other through e-mail.

NAFSA Association of International Education
Rainbow Special Interest Group:

www.indiana.edu/~overseas/lesbigay/student.htm

General information, articles, country guides, scholarships, and personal accounts for gay, lesbian, bisexual, and transgender students.

Financial Aid and Scholarships for Study Abroad

General Information

Federal Student Aid:

www.studentaid.ed.gov

General U.S. Department of Education website about federal financial assistance, including access to the Free Application for Federal Student Aid at www.fafsa.ed.gov.

FinAid Guide to Financial Aid:

www.finaid.com

Information, calculators, and searchable databases for scholarships, loans, savings, military aid, and other types of financial assistance.

International Education Financial Aid:

www.iefa.org

Searchable databases, resources, web links, and message boards for financial aid for both U.S. and international students.

NAFSA Association of International Educators
Financial Aid for Study Abroad:

www.nafsa.org/knowledge_community_network.sec/education_abroad_1/
education_abroad_2/practice_resources_12/getting_started

Articles such as "Financial Aid and Study Abroad: Basic Facts for Students," "Financial Aid Resource for International Education," and "Financial Aid for Study Abroad FAQ" provide general information for financial aid used for studying abroad.

Scholarship and Funding Resources:
www.umabroad.umn.edu/financial/scholarships/index.html
Lists of web resources for scholarships and funding for undergraduate and graduate study abroad, compiled by the Learning Abroad Center at the University of Minnesota.

Study Abroad Funding:
www.studyabroadfunding.org
A website of the Institute for International Education with a searchable database for study abroad funding by country, subject, and other special categories.

Scholarships

Benjamin A. Gilman International Scholarship:
www.iie.org/programs/gilman/index.html
U.S. Department of State scholarships for undergraduate study abroad for students with financial need, with a supplement for study of "critical need" languages.

Boren Awards for International Study:
www.borenawards.org
National Security Education Program grants for undergraduate study abroad to underrepresented countries of critical importance to U.S. interests, with language study of less commonly taught languages. Fellowships for graduate study are also available.

Bridging Scholarships:
www.colorado.edu/ealld/atj/Bridging/scholarships.html
Scholarships for undergraduate study abroad in Japan from the Association of Teachers of Japanese.

Carnegie Endowment for International Peace, Junior Fellow
Program: www.carnegieendowment.org
One-year research fellowships for recent graduates with the endowment's senior associates. The Carnegie Endowment promotes international engagement of the United States and peaceful interaction between nations.

DAAD German Academic Exchange Service:
www.daad.org/?p=46362
Undergraduate scholarships, summer courses, and internships for study abroad experiences in Germany. Graduate and faculty opportunities are also available.

Fulbright Program for U.S. Students:
http://us.fulbrightonline.org/home.html
> Grants from the U.S. Department of State for study, research, or teaching assistantship opportunities abroad for students with a bachelor's degree.

Hispanic Study Abroad Scholars:
www.studyabroadscholars.org
> Study abroad scholarships for students from the Hispanic Association of Colleges and Universities (HACU) member schools.

John T. Petters Foundation:
www.johntpettersfoundation.org
> Scholarships for students studying international business through study abroad programs.

National Science Foundation Graduate Research Fellowship:
www.nsfgrfp.org
> Support for graduate study in the United States and abroad for students pursuing graduate degrees in the sciences, technology, engineering, or mathematics.

Rhodes Scholarships:
www.rhodesscholar.org
> A highly selective program, Rhodes Scholarships offer full fellowships for graduate studies at Oxford University in England.

Rotary International:
www.rotary.org/en/StudentsAndYouth
> Various youth and educational programs and scholarships for international exchange.

Woodrow Wilson National Fellowship Foundation:
www.woodrow.org
> Support for fellowships for teaching and graduate study in foreign affairs, conservation, women and gender, religion and ethics, and access and opportunity.

Country, Region, and City-Specific Information

Atlapedia Online:
www.atlapedia.com
> Maps, facts, and statistics on countries of the world.

CIA World Factbook:
www.cia.gov/cia/publications/factbook
> An online factbook with reference maps, country profiles, flags, and other information for countries and regions of the world.

CountryReports:

www.countryreports.org

A for-fee service providing information on the history, customs, cultures, symbols, geography, economy, population, government, and current events of countries of the world. Includes maps, flags, statistical information, photographs, and a tool for comparison of several countries.

CultureGrams:

www.culturegrams.com

A for-fee service that provides online or print profiles of countries of the world, including the United States.

Michigan State University Global Access:

www.msuglobalaccess.net

A database of websites and other resources searchable by world region or country, thematic area, constituency group, or resource type. Easily accessible country profile pages.

U.S. Department of State Background Notes:

www.state.gov/r/pa/ei/bgn/

Country profiles of the nations of the world including information on the geography, people, culture, history, government, politics, and economy.

World Legal Information Institute:

www.worldlii.org

A free, independent, nonprofit global organization providing legal databases from world countries and regions.

General Cultural Information

Culturosity.com:

www.culturosity.com

Articles, resource lists, links, books, and guides about culture in general, pop culture, and cultural awareness. The website aims to increase global awareness through the discovery of cultures.

Peace Corps Culture Matters Workbook:

www.peacecorps.gov/wws/educators/enrichment/culturematters/index.html

A useful guidebook covering issues of cultural awareness and intercultural communication.

News Resources

International News Sources:
BBC News (http://news.bbc.co.uk), International Herald Tribune
(www.iht.com)
> Some of the many online newspapers and journals read worldwide and covering international news.

Internet Radio and Television:
www.radiofreeworld.com
> Podcasts and Internet radio stations from around the world.

World Newspaper Directories:
www.worldpress.org, www.newsdirectory.com, http://newslink.org,
www.onlinenewspapers.com, www.thepaperboy.com
> Databases and links to online newspapers from countries around the world.

Travel and Tourism Information

The Backpacker:
www.thebackpacker.net
> Reviews of destinations, restaurants, attractions, food, and accommodations from independent travelers and backpackers. A travel wiki allows easy contribution, and stories give firsthand accounts of travelers' experiences.

Eurotrip:
www.eurotrip.com
> Travel advice and savings for travel in Europe from independent travelers. The website features tips by city, with travel-focused discussion forums, maps, podcasts, and links.

Smarter Travel:
www.smartertravel.com
> Articles and tips for inexpensive travel, and search engines for flights, hotels, cars, and cruises.

Tales from a Small Planet:
www.talesmag.com
> Fictional stories, articles, and interactive posts about living in a foreign country.

Time Out City Guides:
www.timeout.com
> Up-to-the-minute information about culture, art, and urban life in a number of world cities.

Tourism Offices Worldwide Directory:

www.towd.com

Links to tourism office websites around the world.

Travel Guides:

Fodor's Travel (www.fodors.com), Frommers Travel Guides (www.frommers
.com), Lonely Planet Travel Guides (www.lonelyplanet.com), Let's Go Travel
Guides (www.letsgo.com), Rough Guides (www.roughguides.com)

Electronic and print travel guides with selections of highlights, photos,
phrasebooks, maps, hotel and restaurant suggestions, stories from travelers,
and cultural information for countries around the world. Both online information and books are for sale on the websites.

Travelmag:

www.travelmag.co.uk

Articles about nontraditional travel destinations by independent travelers,
arranged by destination.

TripAdvisor:

www.tripadvisor.com

Online travel guide based on travelers' reviews and submissions. The website includes a public forum as well as information about worldwide
destinations.

Virtual Tourist:

www.virtualtourist.com

An online travel guide with reviews by travelers themselves. The website
includes guides by city, discussion forums organized by location, and a trip
planner tool.

World Hum:

www.worldhum.com

Dispatches and blogs from travelers around the world, including an FAQ
section, links, and an online store. Articles talk about destinations, but also
the process of traveling successfully.

Practical Tools and Tips for Travel Abroad

Currency Converter:

www.xe.com

A tool to convert one country's currency to another.

Cybercaptive:

http://cybercaptive.com

A cybercafé search engine.

Emergency Numbers Around the World:

www.911dispatch.com/911/911_world.html

Emergency telephone numbers for several countries.

International Calling Codes:

www.countrycodes.com

Easy access to international telephone calling codes around the world.

Packing Tips: One Bag:

www.onebag.com

How to pack less and enjoy the benefits.

Time Zone Calculators:

www.worldtimeserver.com, www.timeanddate.com/worldclock

Calculate the time differences between any two countries of the world.

The Trail Database:

www.traildatabase.org

A worldwide walking and hiking trail database.

Travelite:

www.travelite.org

Useful tips for packing light.

Travlang:

www.travlang.com

Currency converter, translation tool, dictionary, useful phrases, measurement conversions, facts, flags, international road signs, foreign newspapers and radios, and other links, and useful information for travelers.

Travel Regulations and Information

Federal Aviation Administration:

www.faa.gov

Airport and air travel guidelines and regulations.

Federal Voting Assistance Program:

www.fvap.gov

Information about absentee voting from overseas, including absentee ballots.

International Student Identity Card:

www.myisic.com

An internationally accepted identity card for students, good for discounts worldwide as well as a travel insurance plan.

Transportation Security Administration:

www.tsa.gov

Tips to make your check-in and security checkpoint process at U.S. airports go more smoothly. Information for travelers with special needs.

U.S. Customs and Border Protection:
www.cbp.gov/
> Travel tips and news about what to expect when you go through customs in the United States.

U.S. Department of State information on passports and visas:
http://travel.state.gov/passport, http://travel.state.gov/visa

Travel Accommodations and Transportation

Eurail:
www.eurail.com
> Passes to travel through Europe by train at discounted rates. The website also offers travel planning tools and resources.

European low-cost airlines:
Ryanair (www.ryanair.com), Easyjet (www.easyjet.com)
> These airlines offer low-cost flights to European destinations.

Hosteling International (www.hihostels.com), Hostels of Europe (www.hostelseurope.com), Hostels.com (www.hostels.com)
> Search engines for inexpensive lodging for young travelers.

Rail Europe:
www.raileurope.com
> Train tickets and passes, country guides, and train travel information.

STA Travel:
www.statravel.com
> A student travel website offering ticket sales, low-cost ticket options, discount cards, insurance plans, international cell phones, and more.

Student Universe:
www.studentuniverse.com
> An online travel agency for students allowing reservation and purchase of flights, hotels, trains, car rentals, and travel insurance plans.

Ethical and Sustainable Study Abroad and Travel

Better Travel for a Better World from AbroadView:
www.abroadview.org/green/
> Articles by theme and by country, tips, blogs, multimedia, links to web resources, books, and links to organizations about ecologically sound and sustainable travel and study abroad.

Codes of Ethics for Global Tourism:

www.tourismpartners.org/globalcode.html

Guidelines from the World Tourism Organization for sustainable and ethical travel for governments, destinations, tour operators, travel agents, and travelers.

Ethical Traveler:

www.ethicaltraveler.org

News, country information, websites for ethical and sustainable travel, opportunities for action, and guidelines.

Green Passport:

www.greenpassport.us

A pledge to respect the society and environment where you study abroad. This website provides resources for planning your study abroad experience, becoming aware of issues, taking action, advocacy, and reporting. Connect with others in the forum.

Sustainable Study Abroad Resources from Middlebury College:

www.middlebury.edu/academics/ump/sap/sustainable

Steps for a "green" study abroad experience and links to resources for carbon offsets, articles, and websites about sustainable study abroad.

Sustainable Travel International:

www.sustainabletravelinternational.org

Information and programming supporting sustainable and ethical travel and development. The organization provides education and outreach for travelers, travel providers, and other organizations. They also work to develop standards for sustainable tourism and travel practices.

Transitions Abroad Responsible Travel and Ecotourism Resources:

www.transitionsabroad.com/listings/travel/responsible

Responsible travel articles, ecotourism organizations and services, ecotravel books, fair trade resources, information for organizing responsible travel, links to websites.

Working and Volunteering Abroad

AmeriCorps (VISTA Volunteers):

www.americorps.gov

A national service program with a variety of volunteer opportunities throughout the United States. Volunteers pledge a one-year commitment.

Amnesty International:

www.amnesty.org

A worldwide organization promoting human rights internationally through activism and education.

The Carter Center:

www.cartercenter.org

An organization devoted to advancing human rights and promoting peaceful conflict resolution. The Carter Center hosts an internship program for recent graduates.

Catholic Relief Services:

http://crs.org/

An organization serving underprivileged people in foreign countries through advocacy, public policy, education, emergency response, microfinancing, peacebuilding, and other initiatives.

The Chicago Council on Global Affairs:

www.ccfr.org

An organization working to inform leaders and the public of global issues. The council sponsors an internship program for undergraduates.

Greenpeace:

www.greenpeace.org

Organizes environmental activists and offers both volunteer and employment opportunities.

Idealist.org:

www.idealist.org

A database of job opportunities, internships, and organizations in over 165 countries.

International Monetary Fund:

www.imf.org

An international governmental organization bringing together 185 countries to promote financial stability, trade, and cooperation.

Jobs Abroad:

www.jobsabroad.com

A database of international job opportunities, searchable by country or job type.

One Small Planet:

www.onesmallplanet.com/geninfo.htm

Lists of resources for work, travel, internships, and volunteering abroad.

Opportunities for Teaching English as a Foreign Language

EPIK (English Program in Korea):

www.epik.go.kr

The JET Program (Japan Exchange and Teaching):

www.us.emb-japan.go.jp/JETProgram/homepage.html

Knowledge Source (Korea):

www.knowledgesourceus.com

M-ALT (Morioka Assistant Language Teacher) Program in Japan through Earlham College:

www.earlham.edu/~aet

Peace Corps:

www.peacecorps.gov

> Volunteer overseas for two years. The website explains what volunteers do and how to become a volunteer.

Teach Abroad:

www.teachabroad.com

> A database of international teaching opportunities, searchable by country. Resources for teachers include online and teaching English as a foreign language (TEFL) training, strategies, and ideas.

Teach for America:

www.teachforamerica.org

> A corps of recent graduates and professionals committed to teaching in urban and rural public schools in the United States for two years.

United Nations:

www.un.org

> An international governmental organization promoting international peace and security, human rights, humanitarian action, economic development, and international law.

U.S. Department of State Careers Representing America:

www.careers.state.gov/officer/index.html

> Information about careers in the Foreign Service, including job descriptions and how to become a Foreign Service Officer.

Work Gateways:

www.workgateways.com

> Information about working in the United Kingdom including job searches and recruitment agency contacts.

World Bank:

www.worldbank.org

> An international governmental organization providing financial and technical aid to developing countries worldwide.

World Wildlife Fund:

www.worldwildlife.org

> An organization working to protect nature, wildlife, and the environment through field conservation, community action, public policy, and partner-

ship building. The organization sponsors scholarships, grants, and corporate partnerships.

Print Resources

Study Abroad Guides and Handbooks

Dowell, Michelle-Marie, and Kelly Mirsky. *Study Abroad: How to Get the Most Out of Your Experience*. Upper Saddle River, NJ: Prentice Hall, 2003.

Paige, R. Michael, Andrew D. Cohen, Barbara Kappler, Julie C. Chi, and James P. Lassegard. *Maximizing Study Abroad: A Student's Guide to Strategies for Language and Culture Learning and Use*. Minneapolis: University of Minnesota, 2002.

Storti, Craig. *The Art of Coming Home*. Yarmouth, ME: Intercultural Press, 2001.

Advice for Parents

Hoffa, William W. *Study Abroad: A Parent's Guide*. New York: NAFSA: Association of International Educators, 1998.

Culture, Cultural Learning, and Living in a Foreign Country

Althen, Gary. *American Ways: A Guide for Foreigners in the United States*. Yarmouth, ME: Intercultural Press, 2002.

Culture Shock! Series. Portland, OR: Graphic Arts Center Publishing.

DeVita, P. R., and J. D. Armstrong. *Distant Mirrors: America as a Foreign Culture*. Belmont, CA: Wadsworth, 2002.

Gardiner, Harry, and Corinne Kosmitzki. *Lives Across Cultures: Cross-Cultural Human Development*. Boston: Allyn and Bacon, 2007.

Harris, P. R., and R. T. Moran. *Managing Cultural Differences*. Houston, TX: Gulf, 2000.

Hess, Daniel. *The Whole World Guide to Culture Learning*. Yarmouth, ME: Intercultural Press, 1994.

InterAct Series. Boston, MA: Intercultural Press.

Kohls, L. Robert. *Survival Kit for Overseas Living*. Yarmouth, ME: Intercultural Press, 2001.

Lewis, Tom, and Robert Jungman. *On Being Foreign: Culture Shock in Short Fiction*. Yarmouth, ME: Intercultural Press, 1986.

Storti, Craig. *Cross-Cultural Dialogues: 74 Brief Encounters with Cultural Difference*. Yarmouth, ME: Intercultural Press, 1994.

Storti, Craig. *Figuring Foreigners Out: A Practical Guide.* Yarmouth, ME: Intercultural Press, 1999.

Storti, Craig, and L. Bennhold-Samaan. *Culture Matters: The Peace Corps Cross-Cultural Workbook.* Washington, DC: Peace Corps Information Collection and Exchange, US Government Printing Office, 1998.

Intercultural Communication

Bennett, Milton J. *Basic Concepts of Intercultural Communication.* Boston: Intercultural Press, 1998.

Gudykunst, W. B., and B. Mody, eds. *Handbook of International and Intercultural Communication.* Thousand Oaks, CA: Sage, 2002.

Klopf, D. W. *Intercultural Encounters: The Fundamentals of Intercultural Communication.* Englewood, CO: Morton, 2001.

Martin, J. N., T. K. Nakayama, and L. A. Flores, eds. *Readings in Intercultural Communication: Experiences and Contexts.* Boston: McGraw Hill, 2002.

Samovar, L., and R. Porter, eds. *Intercultural Communication: A Reader.* Belmont, CA: Wadsworth, 2003.

Stringer, Donna, and Patricia Cassiday. *52 Activities for Exploring Values Differences.* Yarmouth, ME: Intercultural Press, 2003.

Other Resources for Your Experience Abroad

Bond, Marybeth. *Gutsy Women: Travel Tips and Wisdom for the Road.* Palo Alto, CA: Travelers' Tales Incorporated, 2001.

Johnson, Alexandra. *Leaving a Trace: On Keeping a Journal.* Boston: Little, Brown, 2001.

Oxford, Rebecca L. *Language Learning Strategies: What Every Teacher Should Know.* Boston: Heinle and Heinle, 1990.

Rubin, Joan, and I. Thompson. *How to Be a More Successful Language Learner.* Boston: Heinle and Heinle, 1994.

NOTES

Notes to Chapter 1

1. Benjamin F. Hadis, "Why Are They Better Students When They Come Back? Determinants of Academic Focusing Gains in the Study Abroad Experience," *Frontiers: The Interdisciplinary Journal of Study Abroad* 7 (2002), 57–72; Randi I. Kim and Susan B. Goldstein, "Intercultural Attitudes Predict Favorable Study Abroad Expectations of U.S. College Students," *Journal of Studies in International Education* 9 (2005), 265–279.

2. Institute of International Education (IIE), *Open Doors Report on International Education Exchange 2008,* www.open-doors.iienetwork.org (accessed November 24, 2008).

3. In 2006–2007, for example, 82 percent of U.S. students who participated in study abroad were white/Caucasian and 4 percent were African American; other minorities were significantly underrepresented as well. Institute of International Education (IIE), *Open Doors Report 2008.*

4. Ibid.

5. See J. R. Hopkins, "Studying Abroad as a Form of Experiential Education," *Liberal Education* 85 (1999), 36–41.

6. Institute of International Education (IIE), *Open Doors Report 2008.*

7. Hadis, "Why Are They Better Students When They Come Back?" 57–70.

8. Reflection has its foundations in action research "using naturalistic inquiry including participant observation, dialogic conversation, auto-ethnography, reflective writing, and other methods in classroom research. The conceptual foundations of action research in education can be traced back to the work of John Dewey in the 1920s and subsequent scholarship including experimental work at the Teacher's College of Columbia University in the 1950s." R. Leitch and C. Day, "Action Research and Reflective Practice: Towards a Holistic View," *Educational*

Action Research 8 (2000), 179–193; see also Raka Shome and R. Hegde, "Culture, Communication, and the Challenge of Globalization," *Critical Studies in Media Communication* 19 (2002), 172–189.

9. Larry Braskamp, David Braskamp, and Kelly Carter Merrill, "Global Perspectives Inventory," www.gpinv.org (accessed May 9, 2008).

10. http://www.unesco.org/education/imld_2002/unversal_decla.shtml (accessed August 17, 2008).

11. Angela Kay-yee Leung, William W. Maddux, Adam D. Galinsky, and Chi-yue Chiu, "Multicultural Experience Enhances Creativity: The When and How," *American Psychologist* 63 (2008), 169–181; Chi-yue Chiu and Ying-yi Hong, "Cultural Processes: Basic Principles," in *Social Psychology: Handbook of Basic Principles*, 2nd ed., ed. E. T. Higgins and A. E. Kruglanski (New York: Guilford Press, 1996).

12. Milton J. Bennett, "Intercultural Communication: A Current Perspective," in *Basic Concepts of Intercultural Communication: Selected Readings*, ed. Milton J. Bennett (Yarmouth, ME: Intercultural Press, 1998), 3.

13. Bennett, "Intercultural Communication: A Current Perspective," 12.

14. The iceberg model is attributed to Robert Kohls, *Survival for Overseas Living: For Americans Planning to Live and Work Abroad* (Yarmouth, ME: Intercultural Press, 1996), 29–36.

15. The Pew Global Attitudes Project, "24-Nation Pew Global Attitudes Survey" (Washington, D.C.: June 12, 2008), 3–4.

16. Stephen Brooks, *As Others See Us: The Causes and Consequences of Foreign Perceptions of America* (Peterborough, Canada: Broadview Press, 2006), 35.

17. Pew Global Attitudes Project, "24-Nation Pew Global Attitudes Survey," 24.

18. Hector Tobar, *Translation Nation: Defining a New American Identity in the Spanish-Speaking United States* (New York: Riverhead Books, 2005), 7; Sam Roberts, *Who We Are Now: The Changing Face of America in the Twenty-First Century* (New York: Henry Holt, 2004).

19. Roberts, *Who We Are Now*, 245.

20. Stephen E. Loflin, *Adventures Abroad: The Student's Guide to Studying Overseas* (New York: Kaplan, 2007), 3.

21. Montserrat Guibernau, *The Identity of Nations* (Cambridge: Polity, 2007), 11.

22. Guibernau, *The Identity of Nations*, 10.

23. Bennett, "Intercultural Communication: A Current Perspective," 19.

24. D. R. Drews, L. L. Meyer, and P. N. Peregrine, "Effects of Study Abroad on Conceptualizations of National Groups," *College Student Journal* 30 (1996), 452–461.

25. John Dewey, *Experience and Education* (New York: Simon and Schuster, [1938] 1997).

26. Jeffrey S. Lantis, Kent J. Kille, and Matthew Krain, "The State of the Active Teaching and Learning Literature," in *The International Studies Association Compendium,* ed. Robert Denemark (London: Wiley-Blackwell, 2010); Ken Bain, *What the Best College Teachers Do* (Cambridge, MA: Harvard University Press, 2004); Peter J. Filene, *The Joy of Teaching: A Practical Guide for New College Instructors* (Chapel Hill: University of North Carolina Press, 2005).

27. Richard L. and Shirley A. Ronkowski, "Learning Styles of Political Science Students," *PS: Political Science and Politics* 30, no. 4 (1997), 732–737; Eric Jensen, *Teaching with the Brain in Mind* (Alexandria, VA: Association for Supervision and Curricular Development, 1988); Lynn M. Kuzma and Patrick J. Haney, "And . . . Action! Using Film to Learn About Foreign Policy," *International Studies Perspectives* 2, no. 1 (2001), 33–50; David Kolb, *Experiential Learning: Experience as the Source of Learning and Development* (Englewood Cliffs, NJ: Prentice-Hall, 1984).

28. James E. Stice, "Using Kolb's Learning Cycle to Improve Student Learning," *Engineering Education* 77 (1987), 291–296. In addition, Kolb's experiential learning cycle illustrated the idea that concrete experience coupled with reflection will be assimilated into the formation of abstract concepts and generalizations— this means that by structuring learning objectives we can help focus on a continuous learning spiral. See Richard D. Lambert, ed., *Educational Exchange and Global Competence* (New York: Council on International Educational Exchange, 1994); Chip F. Peterson, "Preparing Engaged Citizens: Three Models of Experiential Education for Social Justice," *Frontiers: The Interdisciplinary Journal of Study Abroad* 8 (2002), 165–206.

29. These are examples of programs that have an important experiential learning component. These and other examples do not represent a specific endorsement of programs.

30. Janet S. Eyler and D. E. Giles, Jr., *Where's the Learning in Service-Learning?* (San Francisco, CA: Jossey-Bass, 1999). For more information on service learning, see the International Partnership for Service Learning and Leadership website at www.ipsl.org.

31. Kathleen M. Weigert, "Academic Service Learning: Its Meaning and Relevance," in *Academic Service Learning: A Pedagogy of Action and Reflection,* ed. Jeffery P. F. Howard and Robert Rhoads (San Francisco, CA: Jossey-Bass, 1998), 3–10; Jeffery P. F. Howard, "Academic Service Learning: A Counternormative Pedagogy," in *Academic Service-Learning: A Pedagogy of Action and Reflection,* 21–30; Mary A. Hepburn, Richard G. Neimi, and Chris Chapman, "Service Learning in College Political Science: Queries and Commentary," *PS: Political Science and Politics* 33, no. 3 (2000), 617–622.

32. Taso G. Lagos, "Global Citizenship—Towards a Definition," Center for Communication and Civic Engagement, http://depts.washington.edu/gcp/pdf/globalcitizenship.pdf (accessed June 1, 2009).

33. Grant H. Cornwell and Eve W. Stoddard, *Globalizing Knowledge: Connecting International and Intercultural Studies* (Washington, DC: Association of American Colleges and Universities, 1999), 32.

34. Richard Slimbach, "The Transcultural Journey," *Frontiers: The Interdisciplinary Journal of Study Abroad* 11 (2005), 205.

35. Ibid., 207.

36. Milton J. Bennett, "Toward Ethnorelativism: A Developmental Model of Intercultural Sensitivity," in *Education for the Intercultural Experience,* ed. R. M. Paige (Yarmouth, ME: Intercultural Press, 1993), 21–71. See also M. R. Hammer and Milton J. Bennett, *The Intercultural Development Inventory (IDI) Manual* (Portland, OR: Intercultural Communication Institute, 2001).

37. Bennett, "Toward Ethnorelativism," 24; Norman Kauffmann, Judy Martin, Henry D. Weaver, and Judy Weaver, *Students Abroad, Strangers at Home: Education from a Global Society* (Yarmouth, ME: Intercultural Press, 1992); see also Adriana Medina Lopez-Portillo, "Intercultural Learning Assessment: The Link Between Program Duration and the Development of Intercultural Sensitivity," *Frontiers: The Interdisciplinary Journal of Study Abroad* 10 (2004), 179–199.

38. See Craig Storti, *Cross-Cultural Dialogues: 74 Brief Encounters with Cultural Difference* (Boston: Intercultural Press, 1994); Gary Weaver, "The Process of Reentry," *The Advising Quarterly* (1994), www.amideast.org/publications/aq/Back_Issues/1994/w94-html/W94Process.htm (accessed May 16, 2008).

39. Rebecca Hovey and Adam Weinberg, "Global Learning and the Making of Citizen Diplomats," in *The Handbook of Practice and Research in Study Abroad: Higher Education and the Quest for Global Citizenship*, ed. Ross Lewin (New York: Routledge, 2009), 33–48.

40. Judy Bates, "The Effects of Study Abroad on Undergraduates in an Honors International Program," doctoral diss. (Columbia: University of South Carolina, 1997).

41. Secretary of State Colin Powell, "Statement on International Education Week 2004" (October 15, 2004), http://www.state.gov/secretary/former/powell/remarks/37137.htm (accessed April 30, 2008).

Notes to Chapter 2

1. For further information, see Resources.

2. Lilli Engle and John Engle, "Study Abroad Levels: Toward a Classification of Program Types," *Frontiers: The Interdisciplinary Journal of Study Abroad* 9 (2003), 1–20.

3. Lynne Bond, Sinan Koont, and Skye Stephenson, "The Power of Being There: Study Abroad in Cuba and the Cultivation of a 'Culture of Peace,'" *Frontiers: The Interdisciplinary Journal of Study Abroad* 11 (2005), 99–120.

4. Grant H. Cornwell and Eve W. Stoddard, *Globalizing Knowledge: Connecting International and Intercultural Studies* (Washington, DC: Association of American Colleges and Universities, 1999), 4.

5. Stephen Ferst, "Go Exotica? Education Abroad to Nontraditional Locations," *International Educator* 16, no. 3 (May–June 2007).

6. Humphrey Tonkin and Diego Quiroga, "A Qualitative Approach to the Assessment of International Service-Learning," *Frontiers: The Interdisciplinary Journal of Study Abroad* 10 (2004), 132–150; Howard A. Berry, "Breaking New Ground: The Impact of International Service-Learning Programs on the Study Abroad Field," in *Study Abroad: 21st Century Perspectives,* ed. Martin Tillman (Stamford, CT: American Institute of Foreign Study Foundation, 2003), http://www.aifs.org/aifsfoundation/21century.htm (accessed July 21, 2008).

7. Mel C. Bolen and Patricia C. Martin, "Introduction: Undergraduate Research Abroad: Challenges and Rewards," *Frontiers: The Interdisciplinary Journal of Study Abroad* 12 (2005), xi–xvi.

8. Janet M. Bennett, "On Becoming a Global Soul: A Path to Engagement During Study Abroad," in *Developing Intercultural Competence and Transformation: Theory, Research, and Application in International Education*, ed. Victor Savicki (Sterling, VA: Stylus Publishing, 2008).

9. Institute of International Education (IIE), *Open Doors Report 2008.*

10. Wendy Shames and Peg Alden, "The Impact of Short Term Study Abroad on the Identity Development of College Students with Learning Disabilities and/or AD/HD," *Frontiers: The Interdisciplinary Journal of Study Abroad* 11 (2005), 1–31.

11. Edward C. Ingraham and Debra L. Peterson, "Assessing the Impact of Study Abroad on Student Learning at Michigan State University," *Frontiers: The Interdisciplinary Journal of Study Abroad* 10 (2004), 83–100. More evidence of the effects of program length on student development can be found in Adriana Medina López-Portillo, "Intercultural Learning Assessment: The Link Between Program Duration and the Development of Intercultural Sensitivity," *Frontiers: The Interdisciplinary Journal of Study Abroad* 10 (2004), 179–200; and Mary M. Dwyer, "More Is Better: The Impact of Study Abroad Program Duration," *Frontiers: The Interdisciplinary Journal of Study Abroad* 10 (2004), 151–164.

12. Lisa Chieffo and Lesa Griffiths, "Large-Scale Assessment of Student Attitudes After a Short-Term Study Abroad Program," *Frontiers: The Interdisciplinary Journal of Study Abroad* 10 (2004), 165–177.

13. William Lenz and Joseph Wister, "Short-Term Abroad with Long-Term Benefits," *International Educator* 17, no. 2 (2008), 84–87.

14. Institute of International Education (IIE), *Open Doors Report 2008*.

15. Norman Segalowitz, Barbara Freed, Joe Collentine, Barbara Lafford, Nicole Lazar, and Manuel Díaz-Campos, "A Comparison of Spanish Second Language Acquisition in Two Different Learning Contexts: Study Abroad and the Domestic Classroom," *Frontiers: The Interdisciplinary Journal of Study Abroad* 10 (2004), 1–18.

16. Institute of International Education (IIE), *Open Doors Report 2008*.

17. Megan Che, Mindy Spearman, and Agida Manizade, "Constructive Disequilibrium," in *The Handbook of Practice and Research in Study Abroad: Higher Education and the Quest for Global Citizenship*, ed. Ross Lewin (New York: Routledge, 2009), 99–116.

18. Examples of study abroad directories include www.studyabroad.com and www.iiepassport.org.

19. See http://www.forumea.org/standards-standards.cfm (accessed October 20, 2009). The Forum on Education Abroad is the Standards Development Organization for study abroad as recognized by the U.S. Department of Justice and the Federal Trade Commission. In addition, the IES MAP (Model Assessment Practice) can be consulted and downloaded from the IES Abroad website at https://www.iesabroad.org/IES/Advisors_and_Faculty/iesMaP.html (accessed October 20, 2009). It was created by a task force of professionals from the field of study abroad as well as experts in student development and assessment.

20. Mobility International USA (www.miusa.org) has information about study abroad for students with disabilities, and they offer assistance and counsel to students wishing to study abroad. The University of Minnesota's Learning Abroad Center also provides resources of the same nature (www.umabroad.umn .edu/access).

Notes to Chapter 3

1. Lilli Engle and John Engle, "Assessing Language Acquisition and Intercultural Sensitivity Development in Relation to Study Abroad Program Design," *Frontiers: The Interdisciplinary Journal of Study Abroad* 10 (2004), 219–236.

2. There are a number of resources providing theory and strategy for language learning: David J. Mendelsohn, *Learning to Listen: A Strategy-Based Approach for the Second-Language Learner* (San Diego: Dominie Press, 1994); Rebecca L. Oxford, *Language Learning Strategies: What Every Teacher Should Know* (Boston: Heinle and Heinle, 1990); Joan Rubin and I. Thompson, *How to Be a More Successful Language Learner* (Boston: Heinle and Heinle, 1994); see also Tracy Rundstrom Williams, "Exploring the Impact of Study Abroad on Students' Intercultural Communication Skills: Adaptability and Sensitivity," *Journal of Studies in International Education* 9, no. 4 (2005), 356–371.

3. Edward T. Hall, *Beyond Culture* (New York: Doubleday, 1976); Edward T. Hall, "The Power of Hidden Differences," in *Basic Concepts of Intercultural Communication: Selected Readings*, ed. Milton J. Bennett (Yarmouth, ME: Intercultural Press, 1998), 53–67.

4. Joseph L. Brockington and Margaret D. Wiedenhoeft, "The Liberal Arts and Global Citizenship," in *The Handbook of Practice and Research in Study Abroad: Higher Education and the Quest for Global Citizenship*, ed. Ross Lewin (New York: Routledge, 2009).

5. Craig Storti, *Cross-Cultural Dialogues* (Boston: Intercultural Press, 1994).

6. Kristi Hanratty, "Full Circle Learning in Study Abroad," *International Educator* 10 (2001), 28–34.

7. Robert L. Kohls, *The Survival Kit for Overseas Living for Americans Planning to Live and Work Abroad* (Yarmouth, ME: Intercultural Press, 1996).

8. Stephanie Budge, "Peer Mentoring in Post-Secondary Education: Implications for Research and Practice," *Journal of College Reading and Learning* 37, no. 1 (2006), 73–87.

9. Don Tapscott and Anthony D. Williams, *Wikinomics: How Mass Collaboration Changes Everything* (London: Penguin Books, 2008).

10. See http://www1.umn.edu/umnnews/Feature_Stories2/Educational_benefits_of_social_networking_sites.html (accessed July 24, 2008).

11. Jeffrey A. Howard, "Why Should We Care About Student Expectations?" in *Promoting Reasonable Expectations: Aligning Student and Institutional Views of the College Experience*, ed. Thomas E. Miller, Barbara E. Bender, and John H. Schuh (San Francisco: Jossey-Bass, 2005), 10–33.

12. Sharon Wilkinson, *Foreign Language Conversation and the Study Abroad Transition: A Case Study,* unpublished doctoral diss. (Harrisburg: Pennsylvania State University, 1995).

13. Vija G. Mendelson, "Hindsight Is 20/20: Student Perceptions of Language Learning and the Study Abroad Experience," *Frontiers: The Interdisciplinary Journal of Study Abroad* 10 (2004), 43–63.

14. Jeffrey A. Howard, "Why Should We Care About Student Expectations?"

15. Anastasia Kitsanta, "Studying Abroad: The Role of College Students' Goals on the Development of Cross-Cultural Skills and Global Understanding," *College Student Journal* (September 2004), http://findarticles.com/p/articles/mi_m0FCR/is_3_38/ai_n6249230?tag=artBody;col1 (accessed August 3, 2008).

16. This information on crisis management is found in the *SAFETI Adaptation of Peace Corps Resources*, http://www.globaled.us/peacecorps/introduction.html (accessed July 22, 2008), as well as the SAFETI website at http://www.globaled.us/safeti/ (accessed October 20, 2009).

17. From the *SAFETI Adaptation of Peace Corps Resources: Crisis Management Workbook*, http://www.globaled.us/peacecorps/crisis_w.html (accessed January 2, 2009).

18. See http://www.anad.org/22385/index.html (accessed July 22, 2008).

19. From a 2004 report of the American College Health Association, http://www.healthyminds.org/cmhdepression.cfm (accessed July 22, 2008).

20. http://www.healthyminds.org/collegestats.cfm (accessed July 22, 2008).

21. From a UCLA study in 2004, according to the National Mental Health Association, http://www1.nmha.org/may/fast_facts.pdf (accessed July 22, 2008).

22. From a 2004 American College Health Association study, according to the National Mental Health Association, http://www1.nmha.org/may/fast_facts .pdf (accessed July 22, 2008).

23. Janet Hulstrand, *What Parents Need to Know! Before, During, and After Education Abroad* (Washington, DC: NAFSA: Association of International Educators, 2007); Bill Hoffa, http://www.studyabroad.com/guides/parentsguide/ (accessed August 7, 2008); *Responsible Study Abroad: Good Practices for Health and Safety*, by the Interorganizational Task Force on Safety and Responsibility in Study Abroad of NAFSA: Association of International Educators, www.nafsa .org/knowledge_community_network.sec/education_abroad_1/developing_ and_managing/practice_resources_36/guidelines_for_health (accessed April 14, 2009).

Notes to Chapter 4

1. There are several theories of cultural development. The stages of intercultural sensitivity appear in Milton Bennett, "A Developmental Approach to Training for Intercultural Sensitivity," *International Journal of Intercultural Relations* 10 (1986): 179–195. The theory of four levels of cultural awareness (unconscious incompetence, conscious incompetence, conscious competence, and unconscious competence) is attributed to William Howell in multiple works, including William Howell, *The Empathic Communicator* (Prospect Heights, IL: Waveland Press, 1986).

2. Milton J. Bennett, "Intercultural Communication: A Current Perspective," in *Basic Concepts of Intercultural Communication: Selected Readings*, ed. Milton J. Bennett (Yarmouth, ME: Intercultural Press, 1998), 1–34.

3. Janet M. Bennett, "On Becoming a Global Soul: A Path to Engagement During Study Abroad," in *Developing Intercultural Competence and Transformation: Theory, Research, and Application in International Education*, ed. Victor Savicki (Sterling, VA: Stylus Publishing, 2008).

4. Bruce LaBrack, "What's up with Culture?" http://www.pacific.edu/sis/ culture/ (accessed January 2, 2009).

5. Peter S. Adler, "The Transitional Experience: An Alternative View of Culture Shock," *Journal of Humanistic Psychology* 15, no. 4 (1975), 13.

6. Janet M. Bennett, "Transition Shock: Putting Culture Shock in Perspective," in *Basic Concepts of Intercultural Communication: Selected Readings*, ed. Milton J. Bennett (Yarmouth, ME: Intercultural Press, 1998), 215–223.

7. Petra Crosby, Margit Johnson, and Eva Posfay, *Coming and Going: Intercultural Transitions for College Students* (Northfield, MN: Carleton College, 2003).

8. John Gullahorn and Jeanne Gullahorn, "An Extension of the U-Curve Hypothesis," *Journal of Social Issues* 19 (1963), 33–47.

9. Bennett, "Transition Shock: Putting Culture Shock in Perspective."

10. Ibid.

11. Craig Storti, *The Art of Crossing Cultures* (Yarmouth, ME: Intercultural Press, 2001).

12. Cultural adaptation and transition have been discussed and studied since the 1960s by researchers such as Kalervo Oberg, John and Jeanne Gullahorn, Milton and Janet Bennett, and many others. Another literature review and a model for cultural identity and transition are discussed as well in Nan M. Sussman, "The Dynamic Nature of Cultural Identity Throughout Cultural Transitions: Why Home Is Not So Sweet," *Personality and Social Psychology Review* 4 (2000), 355–373.

13. Storti, *The Art of Crossing Cultures.*

14. Craig Storti, *Cross-Cultural Dialogues* (Boston: Intercultural Press, 1994); similar themes are explored in LaRay M. Barna, "Stumbling Blocks in Intercultural Communication," in *Basic Concepts of Intercultural Communication: Selected Readings*, ed. Milton J. Bennett (Yarmouth, ME: Intercultural Press, 1998), 173–189.

15. Richard Slimbach, "The Transcultural Journey," *Frontiers: The Interdisciplinary Journal of Study Abroad* 11 (2005), 205–229.

16. Storti, *The Art of Crossing Cultures.*

17. Ibid.

18. Rebecca Hovey and Adam Weinberg, "Global Learning and the Making of Citizen Diplomats," in *The Handbook of Practice and Research in Study Abroad: Higher Education and the Quest for Global Citizenship*, ed. Ross Lewin (New York: Routledge, 2009), 37.

19. Nadine Dolby, "Reflections on Nation: American Undergraduates and Education Abroad," *Journal of Studies in International Education* 11 (2007), 141–156.

20. Bradley J. Titus and Stacey Bolton Tsantir, "Heritage Seeking and Education Abroad: A Case Study," IIE Network, http://www.iienetwork.org/page/97399 (accessed July 21, 2008).

21. John Dewey, *Experience and Education* (New York: Simon and Schuster, [1938] 1997); David Kolb, *Experiential Learning: Experience as the Source of Learning and Development* (Englewood Cliffs, NJ: Prentice-Hall, 1984).

22. Alexandra Johnson, *Leaving a Trace: On Keeping a Journal* (Boston: Little, Brown, 2001).

23. Jane Jackson, "Assessing Intercultural Learning Through Introspective Accounts," *Frontiers: The Interdisciplinary Journal of Study Abroad* 11 (2005), 165–186; Jane Jackson, "Ethnographic Preparation for Short-Term Study and Residence in the Target Culture," *International Journal of Intercultural Relations* 20 (2006), 77–98.

24. Mandy Reinig, "Blogging Abroad," *International Educator* 17, no. 4 (2008), 48–51.

25. http://travel.state.gov/travel/tips/tips_1232.html#drug_offenses (accessed August 24, 2008).

26. http://www.factsontap.org (accessed July 22, 2008).

27. NAFSA's *Guide to Mental Health Abroad* takes a comprehensive look at mental health statistics, symptoms, and considerations for students abroad, http://www.nafsa.org/knowledge_community_network.sec/education_abroad_1/developing_and_managing/practice_resources_36/onsite/best_practices_in_addressing/ (accessed August 28, 2009).

28. Richard J. Light, *Making the Most of College: Students Speak Their Minds* (Cambridge, MA: Harvard University Press, 2001).

Notes to Chapter 5

1. As discussed in Dawn Kepets, *Back in the USA: Reflecting on Your Study Abroad Experience and Putting It to Work* (Washington, DC: NAFSA: Association of International Educators, 1995).

2. Kevin F. Gaw, "Reverse Culture Shock in Students Returning from Overseas," *International Journal of Intercultural Relations* 24 (2000), 85.

3. Alfred Scheutz, "The Homecomer," *American Journal of Sociology* 50 (1944), 369–376.

4. Bruce Labrack, "Top 10 Immediate Reentry Challenges for Students," *International Educator* (May–June 2006), 66–67.

5. Ibid.

6. Michael K. Zapf, "Cross-Cultural Transitions and Wellness: Dealing with Culture Shock," *International Journal for the Advancement of Counseling* 14 (1999), 105–119; see also N. J. Adler, "Re-Entry: Managing Cross-Cultural Transitions," *Group and Organizational Studies* 6 (1981), 341–356.

7. Gary Weaver, "The Process of Reentry," *The Advising Quarterly* (1994), www.amideast.org/publications/aq/Back_Issues/1994/w94-html/W94Process.htm (accessed May 16, 2008); Craig Storti, *The Art of Coming Home*, 2nd ed. (Boston: Intercultural Press, 2003).

8. Weaver, "The Process of Reentry," 23.

9. Study Abroad for Global Engagement Project, University of Minnesota, http://cehd.umn.edu/projects/sage and http://cehd.umn.edu/projects/sage/SAGE%20-%20CIES%20Presentation.pdf (accessed May 14, 2009).

10. D. R. Drews, L. L. Meyer, and P. N. Peregrine, "Effects of Study Abroad on Conceptualizations of National Groups," *College Student Journal* 30 (1996), 452–461.

11. Philip R. DeVita and James D. Armstrong, eds., *Distant Mirrors: America as a Foreign Culture*, 3rd ed. (New York: Wadsworth, 2002), xii.

12. See Larry A. Samovar and Richard E. Porter, eds., *Intercultural Communication: A Reader* (Belmont, CA: Wadsworth, 2000).

13. Rebecca Hovey and Adam Weinberg, "Global Learning and the Making of Citizen Diplomats," in *The Handbook of Practice and Research in Study Abroad: Higher Education and the Quest for Global Citizenship*, ed. Ross Lewin (New York: Routledge, 2009), 33–48.

14. For more information, see www.glimpse.org; www.transitionsabroad.com.

Notes to Chapter 6

1. See Grant H. Cornwell and Eve W. Stoddard, *Globalizing Knowledge: Connecting International and Intercultural Studies* (Washington, DC: Association of American Colleges and Universities, 1999), 32.

2. Phil Gardner, *2006–2007 Recruiting Trends*, CERI: For the Study of Student Transitions, ceri.msu.edu/recruiting/recruiting.html (accessed October 26, 2008).

3. Stevan Trooboff, Michael Vande Berg, and Jack Rayman, "Employer Attitudes Toward Study Abroad," *Frontiers: The Interdisciplinary Journal of Study Abroad* 15 (Winter 2007–2008), 25.

4. S. Bell-Rose and V. Desai, *Educating Leaders for a Global Society* (London: Wiley, 2005), 2; see also www2.goldmansachs.com/our_firm/our_culture/corporate_citizenship/gs_foundation/knowledge_center/docs/Educating_Leaders.pdf (accessed September 10, 2008).

5. As quoted in Trooboff, Vande Berg, and Rayman, "Employer Attitudes Toward Study Abroad," 24.

6. See Andrew Law and Susan Mennicke, "A Notion at Risk: Interrogating the Educational Role of Off-Campus Study in the Liberal Arts," *Frontiers: The Interdisciplinary Journal of Study Abroad* 15 (Winter 2007–2008), 24–29.

7. Mary M. Dwyer, "More Is Better: The Impact of Study Abroad Program Duration," *Frontiers: The Interdisciplinary Journal of Study Abroad* 10 (Fall 2004), 151–163.

8. According to Charlotte West, "Abroad After Graduation, English Style," *International Educator* (January–February 2008), 50–52.

9. For more information, see http://www.borenawards.org/boren_ fellowship.

10. Authors' note: This does not represent an endorsement of these companies or their employment programs.

11. For more information, see www.teachforamerica.org.

12. For more information, see www.americorps.org.

13. For more information, see www.iie.org/Fulbright.

14. www.jetprogramme.org/e/introduction/index.html (accessed October 26, 2008).

15. For more information, see www.peacecorps.gov/masters/.

16. One example is Edward Perkins. Born in the segregated South in 1928, Perkins eventually enlisted in the military and later earned a college degree and a master's in public administration. When he was forty-four-years old, he passed the Foreign Service exam and rose rapidly through the ranks. He earned a Ph.D. in international relations and gained fluency in four languages. In the late 1980s, he served as the Reagan administration's ambassador to South Africa, where he worked closely with regional leaders in the dismantling of apartheid; see interview with Edward J. Perkins, career diplomat and educator, in Christopher Connell, "The Art of Winning Without Fighting," *International Educator* (January–February 2008), 16–19.

17. For more on this, see A. E. Fantini, F. Arias-Galicia, and D. Guay, *Globalization and 21st Century Competencies: Challenges for North American Higher Education* (Boulder, CO: Western Interstate Commission for Higher Education, 2001).

BIBLIOGRAPHY

Adler, N. J. "Re-Entry: Managing Cross-cultural Transitions." *Group and Organizational Studies* 6 (1981), 341–356.

Adler, Peter S. "The Transitional Experience: An Alternative View of Culture Shock." *Journal of Humanistic Psychology* 15, no. 4 (1975), 13–23.

American Council on Education. "Internationalization of U.S. Higher Education: Preliminary Status Report 2000." Washington, DC: American Council on Education, 2000.

Bain, Ken. *What the Best College Teachers Do*. Cambridge, MA: Harvard University Press, 2004.

Barber, Benjamin. "Globalizing Democracy." *American Prospect* 11, no. 20 (2000). http://www.prospect.org/cs/articles?article=globalizing_democracy (accessed May 22, 2008).

Barna, LaRay M. "Stumbling Blocks in Intercultural Communication." In *Basic Concepts of Intercultural Communication: Selected Readings*, ed. Milton J. Bennett, 173–189. Yarmouth, ME: Intercultural Press, 1998.

Bates, Judy. "The Effects of Study Abroad on Undergraduates in an Honors International Program," doctoral diss. Columbia: University of South Carolina, 1997.

Bell-Rose, S., and V. Desai. *Educating Leaders for a Global Society*. London: Wiley, 2005.

Bennett, Janet M. "On Becoming a Global Soul: A Path to Engagement During Study Abroad." In *Developing Intercultural Competence and Transformation: Theory, Research, and Application in International Education*, ed. Victor Savicki. Sterling, VA: Stylus Publishing, 2008.

Bennett, Janet M. "Transition Shock: Putting Culture Shock in Perspective." In *Basic Concepts of Intercultural Communication: Selected Readings*, ed. Milton J. Bennett, 215–223. Yarmouth, ME: Intercultural Press, 1998.

Bennett, Milton J. "A Developmental Approach to Training for Intercultural Sensitivity." *International Journal of Intercultural Relations* 10 (1986), 179–195.

Bennett, Milton J. "Intercultural Communication: A Current Perspective." In *Basic Concepts of Intercultural Communication: Selected Readings*, ed. Milton J. Bennett, 1–34. Yarmouth, ME: Intercultural Press, 1998.

Bennett, Milton J. "Toward Ethnorelativism: A Developmental Model of Intercultural Sensitivity." In *Education for the Intercultural Experience*, ed. R. Michael Paige, 21–71. Yarmouth, ME: Intercultural Press, 1993.

Berry, Howard A. "Breaking New Ground: The Impact of International Service-Learning Programs on the Study Abroad Field." In *Study Abroad: 21st Century Perspectives*, ed. Martin Tillman. Stamford, CT: American Institute of Foreign Study Foundation, 2008. http://www.aifs.org/aifsfoundation/21century.htm (accessed September 4, 2008).

Bolen, Mel C., and Patricia C. Martin. "Introduction: Undergraduate Research Abroad: Challenges and Rewards." *Frontiers: The Interdisciplinary Journal of Study Abroad* 12 (2005), xi–xvi.

Bond, Lynne, Sinan Koont, and Skye Stephenson. "The Power of Being There: Study Abroad in Cuba and the Cultivation of a 'Culture of Peace.'" *Frontiers: The Interdisciplinary Journal of Study Abroad* 11 (2005), 99–120.

Braskamp, Larry, David Braskamp, and Kelly Carter Merrill. "Global Perspectives Inventory." www.gpinv.org (accessed May 9, 2008).

Braskamp, Larry A., L. C. Trautvetter, and K. Ward. *Putting Students First: How Colleges Develop Students Purposefully.* San Francisco: Jossey-Bass, 2006.

Brockington, Joseph L., and Margaret D. Wiedenhoeft. "The Liberal Arts and Global Citizenship." In *The Handbook of Practice and Research in Study Abroad: Higher Education and the Quest for Global Citizenship*, ed. Ross Lewin, 41-52. New York: Routledge, 2009.

Brooks, Stephen. *As Others See Us: The Causes and Consequences of Foreign Perceptions of America.* Peterborough, Canada: Broadview Press, 2006.

Budge, Stephanie. "Peer Mentoring in Post-Secondary Education: Implications for Research and Practice." *Journal of College Reading and Learning* 37, no. 1 (2006), 73–87.

Che, Meghan, Mindy Spearman, and Agida Manizade. "Constructive Disequilibrium." In *The Handbook of Practice and Research in Study Abroad: Higher Education and the Quest for Global Citizenship*, ed. Ross Lewin, 99-116. New York: Routledge, 2009.

Chieffo, Lisa, and Lesa Griffiths. "Large-Scale Assessment of Student Attitudes After a Short-Term Study Abroad Program." *Frontiers: The Interdisciplinary Journal of Study Abroad* 10 (2004), 165–177.

Chiu, Chi-yue, and Ying-yi Hong. "Cultural Processes: Basic Principles." In *Social Psychology: Handbook of Basic Principles*, 2nd ed., ed. A. E. Kruglanski and E. T. Higgins. New York: Guilford Press, 2007.

Commission on the Abraham Lincoln Study Abroad Fellowship Program. "Global Competence and National Needs: One Million Americans Studying Abroad." 2005. http://www.nafsa.org/_/Document/_/lincoln_commission_report .pdf (accessed June 29, 2008).

Connell, Christopher. "The Art of Winning Without Fighting." *International Educator* (January–February 2008), 16–19.

Connor, Walker. *Ethnonationalism: The Quest for Understanding*. Princeton, NJ: Princeton University Press, 1994.

Cornwell, Grant H., and Eve W. Stoddard. *Globalizing Knowledge: Connecting International and Intercultural Studies*. Washington, DC: Association of American Colleges and Universities, 1999.

Crosby, Petra E., Margit Johnson, and Eva Posfay. *Coming and Going: Intercultural Transitions for College Students*. Northfield, MN: Carleton College, 2003.

DeVita, Philip R., and James D. Armstrong, eds. *Distant Mirrors: America as a Foreign Culture*, 3rd ed. New York: Wadsworth, 2002.

Dewey, John. *Experience and Education*. New York: Simon and Schuster, [1938] 1997.

Dolby, Nadine. "Reflections on Nation: American Undergraduates and Education Abroad." *Journal of Studies in International Education* 11 (2007), 141–156.

Drews, D. R., L. L. Meyer, and P. N. Peregrine. "Effects of Study Abroad on Conceptualizations of National Groups." *College Student Journal* 30 (1996), 452–461.

Dwyer, Mary M. "More Is Better: The Impact of Study Abroad Program Duration." *Frontiers: The Interdisciplinary Journal of Study Abroad* 10 (2004), 151–163.

Engle, Lilli, and John Engle. "Assessing Language Acquisition and Intercultural Sensitivity Development in Relation to Study Abroad Program Design." *Frontiers: The Interdisciplinary Journal of Study Abroad* 10 (2004), 219–236.

Engle, Lilli, and John Engle. "Study Abroad Levels: Toward a Classification of Program Types." *Frontiers: The Interdisciplinary Journal of Study Abroad* 9 (2003), 1–20.

Eyler, J. S., and D. E. Giles, Jr. *Where's the Learning in Service-Learning?* San Francisco: Jossey-Bass, 1999.

Fantini, A. E., F. Arias-Galicia, and D. Guay. *Globalization and 21st Century Competencies: Challenges for North American Higher Education*. Boulder, CO: Western Interstate Commission for Higher Education, 2001.

Ferst, Stephen. "Go Exotica? Education Abroad to Nontraditional Locations." *International Educator* (May–June 2007). http://www.nafsa.org/publication.sec/ international_educator_1/ie_may_jun_2007 (accessed September 6, 2008).

Filene, Peter J. *The Joy of Teaching: A Practical Guide for New College Instructors*. Chapel Hill: University of North Carolina Press, 2005.

Forum on Education Abroad. *Standards of Good Practice for Education Abroad*. Carlisle, PA: Dickinson College, 2007. http://www.forumea.org/documents/Forum EAStandardsGoodPrctMarch2008.pdf.

Galston, William A., and Elaine C. Kamarck. *The Politics of Polarization*. Washington, DC: Third Way, 2005.

Gardner, Phil. *2006–2007 Recruiting Trends*. Collegiate Employment Research Institute: For the Study of Student Transitions. East Lansing: Michigan State University/CERI, 2007. www.ceri.msu.edu/recruiting/recruiting.html (accessed October 26, 2008).

Gaw, Kevin F. "Reverse Culture Shock in Students Returning from Overseas." *International Journal of Intercultural Relations* 24 (2000), 83–104.

Goldman Sachs. "Our Firm, Our Culture: Corporate Citizenship." www2 .goldmansachs.com/our_firm/our_culture/corporate_citizenship/gs_ foundation/knowledge_center/docs/Educating_Leaders.pdf (accessed September 10, 2008).

Guibernau, Montserrat. *The Identity of Nations*. Cambridge: Polity, 2007.

Gullahorn, John, and Jeanne Gullahorn. "An Extension of the U-Curve Hypothesis." *Journal of Social Issues* 19, no. 3 (1963), 33–47.

Hadis, Benjamin F. "Why Are They Better Students When They Come Back? Determinants of Academic Focusing Gains in the Study Abroad Experience." *Frontiers: The Interdisciplinary Journal of Study Abroad* 7 (2002), 57–72.

Hall, Edward T. "The Power of Hidden Differences." In *Basic Concepts of Intercultural Communication: Selected Readings*, ed. Milton J. Bennett, 53–67. Yarmouth, ME: Intercultural Press, 1998.

Hall, Edward T. *Beyond Culture*. New York: Doubleday, 1976.

Hammer, M. R., and M. J. Bennett. *The Intercultural Development Inventory (IDI) Manual*. Portland, OR: Intercultural Communication Institute, 2001.

Hanratty, Kristi. "Full Circle Learning in Study Abroad." *International Educator* 10 (2001), 28–34.

Hepburn, Mary A., Richard G. Neimi, and Chris Chapman. "Service Learning in College Political Science: Queries and Commentary." *PS: Political Science and Politics* 33, no. 3 (2000), 617–622.

Holmes, Lowell D., and Ellen R. Holmes. "The American Cultural Configuration." In *Distant Mirrors: America as a Foreign Culture*, 3rd ed., ed. Philip R. DeVita and James D. Armstrong, 4–26. New York: Wadsworth, 2002.

Hopkins, J. R. "Studying Abroad as a Form of Experiential Education." *Liberal Education* 85 (1999), 36–41.

Hovey, Rebecca, and Adam Weinberg. "Global Learning and the Making of Citizen Diplomats." In *The Handbook of Practice and Research in Study Abroad: Higher Education and the Quest for Global Citizenship*, ed. Ross Lewin, 33–48. New York: Routledge, 2009.

Howard, Jeffrey A. "Why Should We Care About Student Expectations?" In *Promoting Reasonable Expectations: Aligning Student and Institutional Views of the College Experience*, ed. Thomas E. Miller, Barbara E. Bender, and John H. Schuh. San Francisco: Jossey-Bass, 2005.

Howard, Jeffery P. F. "Academic Service Learning: A Counternormative Pedagogy." In *Academic Service Learning: A Pedagogy of Action and Reflection*, ed. Jeffery P. F. Howard and Robert Rhoads, 21-30. San Francisco, CA: Jossey-Bass, 1998.

Howell, William. *The Empathic Communicator*. Prospect Heights, IL: Waveland Press, 1986.

Hulstrand, Janet. *What Parents Need to Know! Before, During and After Education Abroad*. Washington, DC: NAFSA: Association of International Educators, 2007.

Ingraham, Edward C., and Debra L. Peterson. "Assessing the Impact of Study Abroad on Student Learning at Michigan State University." *Frontiers: The Interdisciplinary Journal of Study Abroad* 10 (2004), 83–100.

Institute of International Education (IIE). "Open Doors Report on International Education Exchange 2008." http://opendoors.iienetwork.org (accessed November 20, 2008).

Institute of International Education (IIE). "Open Doors Report on International Education Exchange 2007." http://opendoors.iienetwork.org (accessed June 29, 2008).

Institute for the International Education of Students (IES). "IES Model Assessment Practice (2007)." https://www.iesabroad.org/IES/Advisors_and_Faculty/iesMap.html (accessed April 16, 2008).

Jackson, Jane. "Assessing Intercultural Learning Through Introspective Accounts." *Frontiers: The Interdisciplinary Journal of Study Abroad* 11 (2005), 165–186.

Jackson, Jane. "Ethnographic Preparation for Short-Term Study and Residence in the Target Culture." *International Journal of Intercultural Relations* 20 (2006), 77–98.

Jensen, Eric. *Teaching with the Brain in Mind*. Alexandria, VA: Association for Supervision and Curricular Development, 1998.

Johnson, Alexandra. *Leaving a Trace: On Keeping a Journal*. Boston: Little, Brown, 2001.

Kauffmann, Norman, Judy Martin, Henry D. Weaver, and Judy Weaver. *Students Abroad, Strangers at Home: Education from a Global Society*. Yarmouth, ME: Intercultural Press, 1992.

Kepets, Dawn. *Back in the USA: Reflecting on Your Study Abroad Experience and Putting It to Work*. Washington, DC: NAFSA: Association of International Educators, 1995.

Kim, Randi I., and Susan B. Goldstein. "Intercultural Attitudes Predict Favorable Study Abroad Expectations of U.S. College Students." *Journal of Studies in International Education* 9 (2005), 265–279.

Kitsanta, Anastasia. "Studying Abroad: The Role of College Students' Goals on the Development of Cross-Cultural Skills and Global Understanding." *College Student Journal* (September 2004). http://findarticles.com/p/articles/mi_m 0FCR/is_3_38/ai_n6249230?tag=artBody;col1 (accessed August 3, 2008).

Kohls, L. Robert. *Survival Kit for Overseas Living for Americans Planning to Live and Work Abroad*, 2nd ed. Boston: Nicolas Brealey Publishing, 2001.

Kohls, L. Robert. *Survival Kit for Overseas Living: For Americans Planning to Live and Work Abroad*. Yarmouth, ME: Intercultural Press, 1996.

Kolb, David A. *Experiential Learning: Experience as the Source of Learning and Development*. Englewood Cliffs, NJ: Prentice Hall, 1984.

Kuzma, Lynn M., and Patrick J. Haney. "And . . . Action! Using Film to Learn About Foreign Policy." *International Studies Perspectives* 2, no. 1 (2001), 33–50.

Labrack, Bruce. "Top 10 Immediate Reentry Challenges for Students." *International Educator* (May–June 2006), 66–67.

Lagos, Taso G. "Global Citizenship—Towards a Definition." Center for Communication and Civic Engagement. http://depts.washington.edu/gcp/pdf/globalcitizenship.pdf (accessed June 1, 2009).

Lambert, Richard D., ed. *Educational Exchange and Global Competence*. New York: Council on International Educational Exchange, 1994.

Lantis, Jeffrey S., Kent J. Kille, and Matthew Krain. "The State of the Active Teaching and Learning Literature." In *The International Studies Association Compendium*, ed. Robert Denemark. London: Wiley-Blackwell, 2009.

Law, Andrew, and Susan Mennicke. "A Notion at Risk: Interrogating the Educational Role of Off-Campus Study in the Liberal Arts." *Frontiers: The Interdisciplinary Journal of Study Abroad* 15 (Winter 2007–2008), 24–29.

Leitch, R., and C. Day. "Action Research and Reflective Practice: Towards a Holistic View." *Educational Action Research* 8 (2000), 179–193.

Lenz, William, and Joseph Wister. "Short-Term Abroad with Long-Term Benefits." *International Educator* 17 (May–June 2008).

Leung, Angela Kay-yee, William W. Maddux, Adam D. Galinsky, and Chi-yue Chiu. "Multicultural Experience Enhances Creativity: The When and How." *American Psychologist* 63 (2008), 169–181.

Lewin, Ross, ed. *The Handbook of Practice and Research in Study Abroad: Higher Education and the Quest for Global Citizenship*. New York: Routledge, 2009.

Light, Richard J. *Making the Most of College: Students Speak Their Minds*. Cambridge, MA: Harvard University Press, 2001.

Loflin, Stephen E. *Adventures Abroad: The Student's Guide to Studying Overseas*. New York: Kaplan, 2007.

López-Portillo, Adriana Medina. "Intercultural Learning Assessment: The Link Between Program Duration and the Development of Intercultural Sensitivity." *Frontiers: The Interdisciplinary Journal of Study Abroad* 10 (2004), 179–199.

Lutterman-Aguilar, Ann, and Orval Gingerich, "Experiential Pedagogy for Study Abroad: Educating for Global Citizenship." *Frontiers: The Interdisciplinary Journal of Study Abroad* 8 (Winter 2002), 43–82.

Mendelson, Vija G. "Hindsight Is 20/20: Student Perceptions of Language Learning and the Study Abroad Experience." *Frontiers: The Interdisciplinary Journal of Study Abroad* 10 (2004), 43–63.

Mendelsohn, David J. *Learning to Listen: A Strategy-Based Approach for the Second-Language Learner.* San Diego: Dominie Press, 1994.

Oxford, Rebecca L. *Language Learning Strategies: What Every Teacher Should Know.* Boston, MA: Heinle and Heinle, 1990.

Peterson, Chip F. "Preparing Engaged Citizens: Three Models of Experiential Education for Social Justice." *Frontiers: The Interdisciplinary Journal of Study Abroad* 8 (Winter 2002), 165–206.

Pew Global Attitudes Project. "24-Nation Pew Global Attitudes Survey." Washington (June 12, 2008).

Powell, Colin. "Statement on International Education Week 2004." October 15, 2004. http://www.state.gov/secretary/former/powell/remarks/37137.htm (accessed April 30, 2008).

Reinig, Mandy. "Blogging Abroad." *International Educator* 17, no. 4 (2008), 48–51.

Roberts, Sam. *Who We Are Now: The Changing Face of America in the Twenty-First Century.* New York: Henry Holt, 2004.

Ronkowski, Richard L., and Shirley A. Ronkowski. "Learning Styles of Political Science Students." *PS: Political Science and Politics* 30, no. 4 (1997), 732–737.

Rubin, Joan, and I. Thompson. *How to Be a More Successful Language Learner.* Boston, MA: Heinle and Heinle, 1994.

Samovar, Larry A., and Richard E. Porter, eds. *Intercultural Communication: A Reader.* Belmont, CA: Wadsworth, 2000.

Scheutz, Alfred. "The Homecomer." *American Journal of Sociology* 50 (1944), 369–376.

Segalowitz, Norman, Barbara Freed, Joe Collentine, Barbara Lafford, Nicole Lazar, and Manuel Díaz-Campos. "A Comparison of Spanish Second Language Acquisition in Two Different Learning Contexts: Study Abroad and the Domestic Classroom." *Frontiers: The Interdisciplinary Journal of Study Abroad* 10 (2004), 2–18.

Shames, Wendy, and Peg Alden. "The Impact of Short Term Study Abroad on the Identity Development of College Students with Learning Disabilities and/or AD/HD." *Frontiers: The Interdisciplinary Journal of Study Abroad* 11 (2005), 1–31.

Shome, Raka, and R. Hegde. "Culture, Communication, and the Challenge of Globalization." *Critical Studies in Media Communication* 19 (2002), 172–189.

Slimbach, Richard. "The Transcultural Journey." *Frontiers: The Interdisciplinary Journal of Study Abroad* 11 (August 2005), 205–229.

Stice, J. E. "Using Kolb's Learning Cycle to Improve Student Learning." *Engineering Education* 77, no. 5 (1987), 291–296.

Storti, Craig. *The Art of Coming Home*, 2nd ed. Boston: Intercultural Press, 2003.

Storti, Craig. *The Art of Crossing Cultures*. Yarmouth, ME: Intercultural Press, 2001.

Storti, Craig. *Cross-Cultural Dialogues: 74 Brief Encounters with Cultural Difference*. Boston: Intercultural Press, 1994.

Tapscott, Don, and Anthony D. Williams. *Wikinomics: How Mass Collaboration Changes Everything*. London: Penguin Books, 2008.

Titus, Bradley J., and Stacey Bolton Tsantir. "Heritage Seeking and Education Abroad: A Case Study." IIE Network, http://www.iienetwork.org/page/97399 (accessed July 21, 2008).

Tobar, Hector. *Translation Nation: Defining a New American Identity in the Spanish-Speaking United States.* New York: Riverhead Books, 2005.

Tonkin, Humphrey, and Diego Quiroga. "A Qualitative Approach to the Assessment of International Service-Learning." *Frontiers: The Interdisciplinary Journal of Study Abroad* 10 (2004), 132–150.

Trooboff, Stevan, Michael Vande Berg, and Jack Rayman. "Employer Attitudes Toward Study Abroad." *Frontiers: The Interdisciplinary Journal of Study Abroad* 15 (Winter 2007–2008), 25–41.

Weaver, Gary. "The Process of Reentry." *The Advising Quarterly*. 1994. www.amideast.org/publications/aq/Back_Issues/1994/w94-html/W94Process.htm (accessed May 16, 2008).

Weigert, Kathleen M. "Academic Service Learning: Its Meaning and Relevance." In *Academic Service Learning: A Pedagogy of Action and Reflection*, ed. Jeffery P. F. Howard and Robert Rhoads, 3–10. San Francisco, CA: Jossey-Bass, 1998.

West, Charlotte. "Abroad After Graduation, English Style." *International Educator* (January–February 2008), 50–52.

Williams, Tracy R. 2005. "Exploring the Impact of Study Abroad on Students' Intercultural Communication Skills: Adaptability and Sensitivity." *Journal of Studies in International Education* 9, no. 4 (2005), 356–371.

Zapf, M. K. "Cross-Cultural Transitions and Wellness: Dealing with Culture Shock." *International Journal for the Advancement of Counseling* 14 (1999), 105–119.

INDEX

ABOUT THE AUTHORS

Jeffrey S. Lantis is professor of political science and chair of the International Relations Program at The College of Wooster in Ohio. He has extensive international study and travel experience, having recently served as a J. William Fulbright Senior Scholar at the Australian National University. He is the author of books including *The Life and Death of International Treaties* (2009), and numerous articles and book chapters on strategic culture, active teaching and learning in international studies, and foreign policy analysis.

Jessica DuPlaga is the director of Off-Campus Studies at The College of Wooster. She participated in three study abroad programs in France and Belgium, and then worked in academic advising and student services at the IES Nantes Center in France before returning to The College of Wooster in 2007. Living, studying, and working abroad have been an integral part of DuPlaga's undergraduate, graduate, and professional background, and she is devoted to sharing her passion for international education and helping students create positive and purposeful international experiences for themselves.

Mark A. Boyer, University of Connecticut, Series Editor